Pan-Africanism, Pan-Africanists, and African Liberation in the 21st Century: Two Lectures

Published and Forthcoming by New Academia Publishing

PAN-AFRICANISM IN BARBADOS: An Analysis of the Activities of the
Major 20th-Century Pan-African Formations in Barbados
Rodney Worrell

AN ARCHITECT OF DEMOCRACY: Building a Mosaic of Peace
James Robert Huntley

NATIONALISM, HISTORIOGRAPHY AND THE (RE)CONSTRUCTION
OF THE PAST, edited by *Claire Norton*

ASPECTS OF BALKAN CULTURE, *Jelena Milojković-Djurić*

SLAVIC THINKERS OR THE CREATION OF POLITIES, *Josette Baers*

RUSSIAN FUTURISM: A History, *Vladimir Markov*

WORDS IN REVOLUTION: Russian Futurist Manifestoes 1912-1928,
Anna Lawton and Herbert Eagle, eds., trs

IMAGING RUSSIA 2000: Film and Facts, *Anna Lawton*
(CHOICE Outstanding Academic Title 2005)

BEFORE THE FALL: Soviet Cinema in the Gorbachev Years,
Anna Lawton

RED ATTACK, WHITE RESISTANCE: Civil War in South Russia 1918
and
RED ADVANCE, WHITE DEFEAT: Civil War in South Russia 1919-1920
Peter Kenez

Pan-Africanism, Pan-Africanists, and African Liberation in the 21st Century: Two Lectures

Horace Campbell
and
Rodney Worrell

New Academia Publishing, LLC
Washington, DC

Library of Congress Control Number: 2006925192
ISBN 0-9777908-7-8 paperback (alk. paper)

New Academia Publishing, LLC
P.O. Box 27420, Washington, DC, 20038-7420
www.newacademia.com - info@newacademia.com

This book is dedicated to
Leroy Harewood and Ricky Parris.

Contents

Foreword

By Ricky Parris a former Chairman of the Pan-African Movement of Barbados

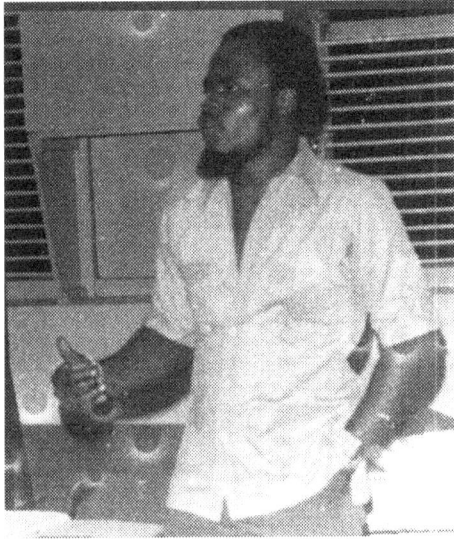

The Pan-African Movement of Barbados (PAMOB) relishes the opportunity to contribute to the ongoing debates on African Liberation struggles. These discussions contribute to a renewal of thinking. The invitation to one of the finest sons of the African Liberation struggle Horace Campbell to deliver the address at the "African Liberation Day Rally & Celebrations 2002" was a special treat. However, to some comrades this lecture turned out to be very controversial. It stirred up enmity in the Black and Brown demagogues and broke the hearts of romantic revolutionary cultural nationalists, but most of all it removed the surrealism and revolutionary mythication and laid the African Liberation struggle bare.

Horace Campbell's address challenged young revolutionaries who seemed stuck in the historical paradigms of the 1960s and the 1970s, in the remembrance of the glorious guerrilla's victories over the brutal European colonial regimes. However, these individuals have not sought to examine the level of revolutionary transformation that has taken place in these former colonial societies. Horace Campbell, a serious scholar of the African Liberation, has much to commend to revolutionaries in his discourse. He calls for a 'firm commitment towards unity of the peoples of Africa away from wars and genocide to peace, love and justice.' Campbell smashed the philosophy that rested on the concept of leaderism; he insisted like Walter Rodney that the first base of any partnership must be with the African peoples, not governments. He was clear that this must be one of the defining aspects of Pan-Africanism and African Liberation in the Twenty-First Century.

Rodney Worrell's "Leroy Harewood" lecture allows us to canonize and pay homage to a revolutionary Barbadian soldier. Through Rodney's pen, one gets a sense of Harewood's prescription for the transformation of the Barbadian landscape. Harewood articulates an alternative path of development that differs significantly from the old, worn path left by the imperialists. His vision was based on a vigorous self-reliant, self-survival initiative, "where the Third World countries would pool their human needs and material resources, so as to become less dependent on the imperialists." Harewood slammed our past leaders for not exhorting us to become pioneers, creators and innovators.

I salute this indomitable, indefatigable fighter of Pan-Africanism and African Liberation, gladdened that Rodney Worrell's analysis brought him close to our hearts.

I commend this book for the erudite study of all functioning revolutionaries interested in African Liberation. Ring the bell, gather all the revolutionaries, come and feed on this discourse, sharpen your ideological armaments and make yourself ready for the battlefield of the twenty-first century: All those who have ears let them hear, all those who have eyes to see, let them see.

Preface

> To talk about Pan-Africanism, to talk about international solidarity within the black world, whichever sector of the black world we live in, we have a series of responsibilities. One of the most important is to define our own situation. A second responsibility is to present that definition to the other parts of the black world, indeed, to the whole of the progressive world. A third responsibility… is to help others in a different section of the black world to reflect on their own specific experience.
>
> *Walter Rodney Speaks:*
> *The Making of an African Intellectual*

In this small work, two comrades, Professor Horace Campbell the veteran Pan-Africanist scholar and Rodney Worrell, a young organic intellectual address some of the burning issues of Pan-Africanism in two lectures in Barbados. The idea to publish these lectures originated with Ricky Parris, the former Chairman of the Pan-African Movement of Barbados who felt that these lectures should be disseminated among the masses of Barbadian people and the African masses globally. Campbell and Worrell readily agreed, but there were a number of challenges that prevented this work from coming out sooner. The untimely death of Ricky Parris was one of the setbacks that delayed this publication.

Campbell in his African Liberation Day address entitled "Pan-Africanism, Pan-Africanists and African Liberation in the Twenty First Century," touched on the following: Africa and international partnerships, defining the task of the 21st century, retreating from the mechanical concepts of humans, leaderism or the lessons of Pan-African struggles in the last century, retreating from wars and violence, African women and liberation, re-conceptualizing Pan-Africanism, Pan-African renewal in the 21st century, USA and their concept of partnering with Africa, reparations and peace in Africa, what kind of Pan-African partnership is possible, whether the Pan-African movement can learn from the lessons of biological warfare, African youths, liberation and peace, and information revolution and peace.

Rodney Worrell in the historic Leroy Harewood Memorial Lecture entitled "Leroy Harewood: Pan-African Humanist," highlights the social and political thought of Leroy Harewood one of unsung heroes of the Caribbean. Unfortunately, many working class West Indians have made sterling contributions in the quest for social justice but their contributions have never been recognized. However, Rodney Worrell seeks to address this deficiency by bringing to the attention of readers, Harewood's views on several issues that are still relevant, including: who are Africans, hunger and underdevelopment, Pan-African solidarity, failure of Barbadian political leaders, shortcomings of the black middle class, Clement Payne/NDP alliance, smashing the neo-colonial state, weaknesses of the liberal democratic model, Caribbean unification, re-colonization and the revolutionary potential of Barbadians.

Finally, there is an appreciation to an outstanding Pan-Africanist.

We thank Ricky Parris for fighting valiantly to see this project completed and for writing the foreword to this publication. Special thanks to Viola Davis and Wynel Appelwaithe for their editorial assistance and support. We must also thank Joy Workman, Angela Brandon-Hall, Annette Maynard-Watson, Mark Adamson, Mark Seale, Chris Oliver, Achirri Adams and David Denny for their support in this project and Dr. Ian Boxill, the editor of *IDEAZ*, for publishing an abridged part of the lecture on Leroy Harewood. We hope that that this publication will educate, enlighten and stimulate.

Pan Africanism and African Liberation in the 21st Century

By Horace Campbell
Lecture delivered to the Pan African Movement of Barbados, African Liberation Day, May 25, 2002, Israel Lovell Foundation 2002

In 2001, I attended the Henry Sylvester Williams Conference, at the University of the West Indies, St. Augustine, Trinidad, where I met Professor Horace Campbell, the Jamaican born Pan-African scholar. I was very impressed by his scholarship and I felt that Barbadians should have the benefit of hearing Professor Campbell speak about Pan-Africanism and African Liberation in the Twenty First Century. On my return to Barbados, I suggested to the members of the Pan-African Movement of Barbados that we should invite Professor Campbell to give the African Liberation Day address 2002. This idea was accepted by the Chairman of the Pan-African Movement of Barbados, Ricky Parris, and supported by other comrades. Professor Campbell gladly accepted the invitation and delivered the African Liberation Day Lecture and rally on the 25th of May, 2002 at the Israel Lovell Foundation.

Introduction of speaker by Rodney Worrell

Introductory greetings

First, I want to thank the members of the Barbados Community for the warmth and generosity that have been offered since I arrived on Wednesday evening. I want to thank in particular the Pan African Movement of Barbados for the efforts to bring me to this beautiful space and I have enjoyed the full range of activities associated with the Pan African Movement of Barbados. I want to thank sister Viola Davis for her hospitality, kindness and patience and the voice that she brings to the movement at this moment. I want to especially thank Brother Rodney Worrell who has been seeking to find ways for me to be part of this discussion on the ways forward for Pan-Africanism in the Eastern Caribbean. I was very pleased to be associated with the launch of his book entitled, *Pan-Africanism in Barbados: An Analysis of the Major 20th century Pan- African Formulations in Barbados.*

The government and peoples of Barbados have been very active in the discussions of Pan Africanism for the past ten years and the representatives of the Commission for Pan-African Affairs and the University of the West Indies at Cave Hill have the basic documents of the World Conference Against Racism process. This process started after the Second World Conference Against Racism (that placed the issue of apartheid at the center of the international politics). The Third WCAR has placed the issues of racism, xenophobia and reparations at the forefront of the new struggles. This process is continuing and there are individuals and organizations in Barbados who are working diligently to ensure that the Program of Action is implemented. There are plans for the follow up of the African Descendants Caucus and there are many different forces in the Pan-African and anti-racist and black women communities that are looking forward to participating in reshaping the issues of anti-racism and reparations.

My greetings are in the traditions of those who represent the variant of Pan Africanism that seek dignity and respect for human life.

Introduction. International context

At the Organization of African Unity (OAU) summit in Lusaka, in July 2001, the Heads of State agreed that the necessary steps would be taken in the transformation of the Organization of African Unity (OAU) into the African Union (AU). In July of this year in South Africa, the African Union will officially be launched, replacing the OAU. The Constitutive Act of the African Union spells out the process for the establishment of unity, solidarity, the defense of the independence of African peoples and governments. There will be:

Assembly of Heads of States

Committees—specialized technical committees of the Union

Councils of the Union—Economic, Social and Cultural

Court—Court of Justice of the Union linked to the International Criminal Court

Executive Council, representing the Council of Ministers

Parliament, representing the people

African Central Bank—linking the financial Institutions of the Union.[1]

The coming together of the African Union will be one of the most important achievements of the Pan-African Liberation struggle in the 21st Century. The goals of the African Union are clear and represent a firm commitment towards the unity of the peoples of Africa away from wars and genocide to peace and love, justice. The main forces for dignity, economic change and gender equality recognize that there must be peace in order for transformation and reconstruction to take place.

Less than a week after the close of the WCAR in Durban when there was the signal of the oppressed peoples of Africa and Asia that they wanted to move humanity in a new direction, two civilian aircrafts were flown into the World Trade Center in New York City in the USA. The use of civilian aircraft as missiles in the attack on the World Trade Center and the Pentagon brought a new kind of warfare into international politics. The government of the USA declared that the attack was an act of terrorism. The political leadership of the USA launched an international war against terrorism.

President George Bush of the USA took the lead to organize an international coalition and embarked on a global crusade to fight terrorism, despite the reality that there was no international consensus on what constituted terrorism. Africans throughout the world felt strong solidarity with all of those who lost their lives at the World Trade Center because Africans know pain and suffering and empathize with those in pain. This is the basic principle of African love, charity and sense of social collectivism.

The leading spokespersons and planners for the USA military industrial complex declared that there would be many phases of the war against terrorism, essentially a war without borders. The peoples of Africa were to be drawn in this global war in many ways. The peoples of the Caribbean, Central and South America will be drawn into this war in so far as one of the principal areas of conflict will be in the Columbia region (as laid out in Plan Columbia). Despite the oppressive conditions of life for the millions of poor people all over the world, billions of dollars are being diverted into war making efforts. War speeds up the processes of transformation and regression and sharpens the understanding of the laws of unforeseen circumstances. It is well known that the dynamics of war cannot be controlled, so it is better to seek-non-military solutions than to escalate the arc of warfare across the globe.[2]

In the international media, especially the Anglo-American media, the images of fighting and military mobilization dominated the airwaves to the point where the main sources of information were saturated with sounds and sights of warfare, violence and 'fighting terrorism.' In the fight against terrorism, it was declared that there was an 'axis of evil' and the world was warned that all peoples and countries had to take sides. Citizens of the world and governments were either aligned with the government of the USA or they were sympathetic to terrorism. In this dividing line, there was little space left for those who called for healing and a retreat from the militarist and masculinist ideas of those who carried out terrorism, and those who were fighting terrorism. At this very same time, Africans at home and abroad were establishing another priority, that of eradicating centuries of exploitation and racism. Africans everywhere are opposed to terrorism whether committed by governments, or committed by movements opposed to governments.

The African Liberation Movement, the peace movement and most of those who want a new international system, remain opposed to the unilateral definitions of terrorism that emanate from the USA and Britain. Africans remember the period of the eighties when the US political and military leaders who are now declaring the war on terrorism considered Osama Bin Laden, the Contras in Nicaragua and Jonas Savimbi freedom fighters. Africans such as Nelson Mandela, and others fighting for African liberation, were considered terrorists. There are numerous books, articles, research institutes and organizations focused on terrorism, but the African liberation experiences dictate that the very same forces that are waging the present war on terrorism must be self critical on their past role. Usually, military force is reserved for the morally weak.

At the present moment, the government of the United States is isolated on many issues in the court of international political opinion. Among the allies of the USA, there is an effort to manage the disagreements because these disagreements are so fundamental and contain the indications of deep-seated capitalist competition. The principal and public disagreements relate to the Kyoto Treaty, the International Criminal Court, the Anti-ballistic Missile Treaty, the Treaty of Non-Proliferation of Nuclear Weapons (NPT), trade issues in relation to subsidies for agriculture, steel and numerous products, disagreements over Palestine, and disagreements over the unilateral deployment of troops. Behind these public disagreements lie the even more fundamental disagreement over future of the International Monetary Fund (IMF) and the World Bank, disagreements over the US dollar as the currency of World trade and disagreements over the global deployment of US troops and the use of religious formulations such as 'the Axis of Evil.' African and Caribbean peoples as well as all peoples must grasp these disagreements to ensure that when struggles break out in the open, oppressed countries are not brought in as cannon fodder.

Inside the USA, the African peoples, the First Nation Peoples and the majority of the peoples of color are following the open disagreements between the US government and the supposed allies. There is a clear awareness on the ways in which the war on terror has been used to increase the erosion of basic rights. In particular, the black peoples and other peoples of color have joined with the Civil Liberties Union in being critical of the legislation that has been passed for Homeland Security. The US Patriot Act (HR 3162, 2001) must be studied by all forces in the world that support the basic human rights of Africans and other peoples who suffer from racial profiling. Breathing while black (as a result of environmental racism), driving while black (as a result of racial profiling), has now been supplemented by flying while Brown. The persecution of peoples of Middle Eastern background and the violation of basic human rights are increasing daily under the guise of fighting terrorism. Throughout the world all peoples are being called upon to forget the burning problems of AIDS, poverty, third world debt, global warming, the Kyoto treaty so that the issues of one country become the primary issue for all countries. The massive military budget (2002) of the USA of over US $379 billion strengthens the producers of weapons of the military industrial complex at precisely the moment when the government is cutting expenditure on education, health, pensions and those entitlements that arose from the New Deal (1930's), the workers' struggles, the civil rights and women's movement. The government has demonized poor African American Women and passed legislation to cut welfare while increasing corporate welfare.

Many of the youths of the African population face a future of prison because of oppressive conditions that they face in every sphere of life. Though the media presents life in the USA as being one of opportunity for those who work hard, the oppression of the African American youth has intensified to the point where the prison system and the criminal justice system are introducing a new kind of slavery. Angela Davis has been in the forefront of the call for the abolition of this new kind of enslavement. [3] From the time of kindergarten, the educational system begins the preparation to send black youths on the paths to prison. There are many black organizations fighting the growth of the prison industrial complex and the fight against the death penalty is one aspect of the struggles of the prison movement. Over the past ten years, the fight to save the life of Mumia (Abu-Jamal) has mobilized the energies of the progressive forces along with Pan-Africanists.

The Black Radical Congress (BRC) is an integral part of the campaign to "Free Mumia" and the BRC has initiated a campaign of *Education not incarceration*.[4] This organization is also dedicated to supporting reparations, justice and peace.

As a member of the BRC from the Pan-Africanist wing we are very aware of the tide of conservatism and racism that is sweeping Western Europe at precisely the moment when the forces aligned against globalization are seeking new forms of solidarity and thinking through the fact that another world is possible. The BRC supports the struggles for self-determination of the peoples of Palestine and the self-determination projects of peoples all around the world.

As we speak, the arrest of those suspected of terrorism is being carried out in a climate where the US government has mooted the prospect of military tribunals. Africans and peace loving persons everywhere must call for the proper legal rights for all. Under the cloud of war, there is the justification that the fight against terrorism requires global war and the loss of civil liberties. It is precisely this climate of repression and sable rattling that emboldens militarists and dictators all over the world. Peace loving people everywhere must call on the governments of India and Pakistan to seek a peaceful resolution to the question of Kashmir. Pan-Africanists everywhere are now challenged to take a clear position on peace in Africa as a component of world peace.

Africans and international partnerships

The warfare and global insecurity generated by the mobilization and preparation for war engulfed the energies of most of humanity at precisely the moment when the African peoples were searching for institutions and organizations in the aftermath of the removal of the apartheid government, the overthrow of the Mobutu government in Zaire and the recent news of the death (in battle) of Jonas Savimbi.[5] Throughout Africa there was the simultaneity of the struggles for peace and reconstruction (from Eritrea and Ethiopia, stretching across the Sudan to Sierra Leone and

Liberia, down through Angola across the Congo to Burundi and Rwanda) even while the question of unfinished issue of colonial occupation remained in the Western Sahara and in the Comoros area of the Indian Ocean. The articulation of the desire for peace has been clearly expressed in the Constitutive Act of the African Union.

The New Partnership for African Development (NEPAD) was launched in 2001 by a triumvirate of African leaders from Nigeria, Senegal and South Africa, as one component of building the African Union. From the period of colonialism there had been numerous calls for continental African Unity, but the forces of repression and destabilization had prevailed from the period of the assassination of Patrice Lumumba in 1961 up to the period of militarism and destruction unleashed by apartheid and a constellation of militarists. Leaders such as Kwame Nkrumah had been most insistent that *Africa Must Unite*.[6] There were numerous forces in Africa calling for an African Union long before the African leadership caught up to be in step with the principles of unity and peace coming from the peoples. Those who seek to discredit the efforts towards the African Union, link the Union to the activities of the President of Libya, Muammar Gaddafi. There is no doubt that President Gaddafi played a positive and important role in convening the meetings to accelerate the push for Union, but to call the African Union the brainchild of Gaddafi is to negate the painstaking work of Pan-Africanists for over one hundred years.

Cultural artists within and outside of Africa sang songs calling for African Unity. Bob Marley was the most popular of these artists, who sang:

> How good and how pleasant it would be
> Before God and Man
> To see the Unification of All Africans.
> Africa Unite.

Bob Marley's call for unity and emancipation was understood in all languages and all societies. Fela Anikulapo-Kuti was one of the many passionate cultural artists that carried the message of Pan-African Unity in a more forceful manner than politicians and radical intellectuals.[7] One of the challenges of this period is for movements and organizations and organic intellectuals of the people to develop new techniques of communication to keep in step with the dynamism and creativity of the popular forces. The ordinary people had long believed in the concept of Africa for the Africans and had been moving across borders with impunity for decades.

Once the political leaders caught up to the spirit of Pan-Africanism from below and formulated the *Constitutive Act of the African Union*, sections of the current leadership sought to give meaning to the process of building Unity.[8] The foundation of the African Union had been premised on a many-sided process of reconstruction that was linked to the NEPAD Initiative and the basic building block for the African Economic Union.[9]

When the leaders of Nigeria, Senegal and South Africa agreed on NEPAD, the collective agreement was inspired by the desire for peace and reconstruction and moving Africa from poverty to prosperity. The details of the Initiative along with the goals are still contested, as social movements and people's organizations in Africa consider the focus of the initiative misguided since it is addressed primarily to Western governments and representatives of international private capital. Many of these organizations that are called Civil Society Organizations (CSO's) are using regional meetings, local radio and community meetings to express their view that the first base of any partnership must be with the African peoples.

The basis of partnership must be on mobilizing the cultural wealth and the multiplicity and diversity of many social forces: the old, the young, women, the believers, the non believers, royalists, professionals, traders, workers, merchants, traditional healers, people of different origins along with those who have settled and made Africa their home. Grassroots activists are not only critiquing the present document but are saying that stakeholders in the African Union must seize the opportunity to make this new start for Africa realized by doing things differently from what has been done before.[10] There are some sections of the African civil society formation that are calling first and foremost for partnerships with the African peoples at home and abroad.

This partnership of peoples and not governments will be one of the defining aspects of Pan-Africansim and African liberation in the twenty first century. All of the indications from the energies and meetings of the new cadre of activists are that this new Pan-African partnership will be grounded on the principles of reparations, peace and justice. Strategic planners for imperial countries who make long term plans for the world economy in the twenty first century view the vast resources of Africa for the revitalization of the global capitalist economy in the 21st century, this is regardless of the fact that millions of Africans are being wiped out by pandemics, war and death from poverty. Africans have to organize their own short term, medium term and long-term plans for the century to end the pessimism that is promoted by those leaders who say that there is no alternative to the western domination.

Defining the tasks of the 21st century

The most important short-term task is for the validation of the lives of Africans. As we in different parts of the African world take stock of the tasks for the 21st century, we have the opportunity to look back and reflect on the tasks of liberation in the last one hundred years. In the process of defining the new tasks it becomes necessary to start from the basic recognition that African life is precious and that the well being of the people comes before land and the power of leaders. The deplorable nature of human existence is manifested in all spheres of social relations and is most evident when one examines the conditions of African peoples globally. The solidarity between peoples who are oppressed developed over the last century in relation to the struggle for dignity in all parts of the African world. The period of Bandung in 1955 (the coming together of peoples of Africa and Asia), at the height of the anti-colonial revolts had ignited and strengthened the movements for independence all over Africa. These movements had earlier gained inspiration from Pan-African students and intellectuals.

The consolidation of Pan-African solidarity was evident in many instances from the period of the Garvey movement (1920's) down to the international campaign against apartheid. These moments in relation to the struggles for dignity reinforced and nurtured positive identification with Africa. There was an underlying theme throughout the century that, 'the people of one part of Africa are responsible for the freedom and liberation of their brothers and sisters in other parts of Africa and indeed the task of black people everywhere was to accept this responsibility.'[11] It was this dictum that inspired the spirit of Pan-African thought and action in the USA throughout the last century.

Over the past one hundred years the conception of liberation has gone through definite stages from the demand for self determination, to the demand for economic freedom, political independence, regional economic integration, democratization, the end to genocide, reparations, the emancipation of women, the humanization of the male and the humanization of the planet. At the end of the century, the conquest of state power by the forces fighting against apartheid in Southern Africa brought an end to that phase of liberation where the liberation was understood simply as the liberation movement raising the flag and gaining a seat at the United Nations. There has been the same disillusionment in Eritrea where the promise of social transformation has been shattered by militaristic rule. It is now clearer that in the main, decolonization and Pan-African liberation was formalized to mean that African males entered the corridors of the old oppressive regime and sought to use this apparatus as the vehicle for creating spaces for a new class. By the end of the twentieth century, the organized African women's movement had redefined the tasks of liberation and broadened the questions of freedom to include the freedom from all forms of oppression. Radical feminists from all four corners of Africa are raising the questions of sexuality, rape, reproductive health and the dangers of deformed masculinity.[12]

The questions that are being forced on the agenda are not new, but had been muted in the all class nationalist period of decolonization. In the process, the new tasks are fundamentally different from the old debates on great revolutionary leaders. Thus, no discussion on Pan-Africanism in the present period can go on without the input of African feminists. This writer identified five main elements of the Pan African struggles that emerged from one such discussion in Trinidad in 2001:

i) The struggles of Africans everywhere to fight for the provision of adequate and accessible health care, especially in the context of the AIDS pandemic. The struggle is also to bring a coordinated global campaign against this disease.

ii) The struggles for peace and reconstruction in the context of the African Union, ending militarism and militarization.

iii) The need for Pan-Africanists to support the struggles

of women in the fight against sexism and all forms of violation and violence.

iv) Reparations.

v) Struggling against the modern manifestations of
plunder and domination as manifest in the World Trade
Organization (WTO), World Health Organization (WHO),
the International Monetary Fund (IMF) and modern institutions of imperialism.[13]

These five core issues emerged from the myriad of questions that must be tackled with new skills and new forms of
organization. Increasingly, it is becoming clearer that the old
forms of analysis, old forms of organization and the conceptual basis of the politics of liberation had been flawed. However, it was not possible to learn these lessons before ex-
hausting the old patriarchal model of liberation. This lesson
in South Africa reinforced the lessons from Algeria, Kenya,
Mozambique, Angola, Zimbabwe and Namibia and all of
the societies where the working poor made major sacrifices
for the armed struggles for liberation. [14]

It was a simple lesson that the colonial state could not be
used as the basis for emancipation. In many parts of Africa,
the fact that the same leaders who were at the forefront of
the Pan-African movement are at the forefront of repression,
ensure that many African women do not want to associate
themselves with Pan-Africanism in the way it is presently
formulated by the leaders of yesterday. The youths are even
clearer in their intention to form a new basis for community
solidarity and peoples' cooperation away from the politics
of exclusion and the ideological illnesses of the past generation.

This challenge of doing things differently and focusing
on African Knowledge and self-reliance principles has been
a theme put forward at meetings in all corners of Africa,
especially at women meetings. These meetings critique the

negative direction of the present leadership that focuses on the further integration of Africa into an unjust social system that has been the source of insecurity since colonialism and the partitioning of Africa. The positions of African workers, scholars, grassroots organizations and civil society organizations continue to be clearly different from the leaders of the Group of 7, and international organizations such as the World Bank and the IMF, that believe the African Union can be an instrument for fighting 'poverty' without the end of the structural imbalances and inequalities of the global system of capitalism.

The majority of Africans who had always been singing and pleading for African Unity have some clarity on the balance of international military and political forces and stress the fact that the positive aspects of African partnerships (such as NEPAD) must be embraced so that there can be an African project that is quite independent of the project of international capital.[15] These social forces that are engaged in the deliberations of how to break the long history of genocide, disease, war and economic exploitation, agree with the positive aspects of NEPAD that spell out the determination of the peoples and leaders of Africa to move to a new era of international cooperation beyond the history of militarism, imperial partitioning, and plunder.[16] The program of Action for the implementation of NEPAD centralizes peace, security, and democracy as the fundamental building blocks for the economic transformation of the conditions of the African peoples.

It is this same Pan-African principle of people's rights and security that is at the base of the search for peace and renewal in Africa. Regional wars, the looting of natural resources, ethnic and religious manipulations and the multiple sources of insecurity in Africa reinforced the position that wars and militarism in one region will infect other states and peoples in that region. Just as wars in Palestine and other parts of the Middle East will negatively affect Africa, wars in Colombia will negatively affect the whole of the Caribbean region. Pan-African conceptions of peace have (in the past) been based on state security and not on the basis of the well being of people or *people's security*. The concept of *people's security* starts from the rights of the people, rights for workers and small farmers, environmental rights, gender equality, women's rights and the rights of children and moves away from the sterile concepts of state security and state sovereignty.

Independence and decolonization for the producers (workers, small farmers, traders, patriotic business persons etc.,) should have meant a transformation of the colonial state and a better standard of living. However, these expectations were dashed because for the assimilated and educated, independence meant inheriting the levers of coercion and administration. There was no major effort to counteract the legacies of force, coercion, low prices for crops and the devaluation of African labor power. Not only had the emergent political elite internalized the ideas of modernization but the ideas of ethnic legitimacy and tribal rivalry had become so pervasive that African leaders have developed a high tolerance for political careerists who rule on the basis of fear and the promotion of genocidal violence.

Pan-Africanism and the anti-colonial struggles in the 21st century

The general deprivation of the producers had reached a point where there was a spate of commentaries that sought to argue that Africans were better off under colonialism. These apologists for colonial rule invoke these ideas in the context of those (anti-colonial forces) who raise the issues of the twenty-three colonies with African people where they do not have the right to national sovereignty. From New Caledonia in the Pacific, to Martinique in the Caribbean, from French controlled Cayenne to the US colony of Puerto Rico and across to the Western Sahara (in Africa) the issue of political independence has not been resolved. Usually, the size of these colonial societies is brought forward and used as an argument against decolonization. The supporters for imperial rule also contend that the standard of living of the colonized peoples (in Martinique and Puerto Rico) is better than the standard of living in the independent Caribbean states (such as Haiti and Jamaica).

Additionally, in the contemporary debates on sovereignty and autonomy of nations, there are some who will say that the principle of political independence is meaningless in the era of the World Trade Organization (WTO) and the globalization of capital. However, for those who suffered oppression, giving in to one form of domination and oppression is only opening the door and inviting other forms of oppression. Those who have been able to defend their independence must develop new ways to support those under colonial rule. This includes raising the questions at the United Nations, at the Organization of American States (OAS) at the African Union, at Caricom, at meetings of African Americans and at other fora where African men and women come together to chart a new path forward. In this process of widening the anti-colonial terrain of the struggle, it will be possible to move from the insistence on armed struggles as the only form of struggle for these societies to escape British, French and United States imperial domination. One other major lesson of the last century was the limitation of the glorification of armed struggles.

The mystique of armed struggles for liberation evaporated as *military entrepreneurs* such as Charles Taylor in Liberia, the Revolutionary United Front in Sierra Leone and the late Jonas Savimbi in Angola used armed guerrillas to terrorize ordinary persons. The history of rampant militarism and the violence that shattered the Algerian, Angolan and Zimbabwean societies, along with the general low respect for human life, has led many to rethink the idea that armed struggles were necessarily superior to social transformations through democratic, peaceful, and persuasive or long drawn out negotiations for change. These experiences from Algeria to South Africa brought about an awareness of the end of the glorification of the armed struggle as the model of liberation. There were many examples of this glorification of violence and the intervention of African feminists in the discussion on liberation helped to smoke out and expose the anti-worker, sexist, male chauvinist, tribalist and homophobic politics of leaders who once saw themselves at the forefront of the liberation movement.

The end of the recent models of civil rights and independence has sharpened the understanding of the strengths and weaknesses of the conceptualizations of liberation. These lessons in the context of changed international politics have further clarified the characterization of Pan-African thought and action for emancipation, as opposed to Pan-Africanism for the capture of state power. These modes of thought and action form part of the framework for human renewal and for a recovery of the human spirit, away from the mechanical notions of humans as living machines. At the end of the century the rapid technological changes reinforced the need to step back and place humanity and human needs at the centre of human relations.

Retreating from mechanical concepts of humans

In the context of the contemporary stress on force and militarism in the world, this inquiry is inspired by the importance of raising the question of Africa and the possibilities to move from the era of dehumanization, to one where the dignity of the human spirit is affirmed. Leaders and governments that saturate their societies with cultural products from imperial countries have overshadowed the real cultural unity of the peoples. Embedded in these cultural products, especially in the language and education of former colonial countries are racist depictions of Africa and African peoples. The principal theme of recovering the dignity of the black person continues to dominate the concept of liberation. Africans in all parts of the planet live within the shadow of the experiences of slavery, genocide, and lynching and institutionalized racism.

The experiences of genocide are represented in Western societies as acts of civilizing and pacifying 'barbaric' Africans. 'Pacification' followed from the experience of the Atlantic slave trade and the reverberations of this trade in human beings continue to register a negative impact on humanity. This slave trade took place in the same period as the scientific and technological revolution that accelerated the transformation from feudalism to capitalism.

Africans from the continent were captured, placed in chains, and dispersed as the global reach of Western Europe opened new spaces for capital accumulation. In this sense, the present globalization is not new for Africans. The global reach of capitalists in Europe was spread and justified in the name of 'progress.' The scientific advances of the 'European Enlightenment' were presented as manifestations of the rationality and superiority of Europeans. It was not insignificant that the principal thinkers of Western Europe were inspired to develop theories of the market, the individual and the property relations in the heady days of the rapid accumulation of wealth in the context of the trade in human beings. Adam Smith, one of the pre-eminent articulators of western economic thought, considered Africans as less than human beings and black women as being no better than prostitutes.[17] Sexism, patriarchy, the ideas of private property, male centered inheritance and the market were universalized as values of human nature. During the industrial revolution science and technology developed a firm base in production and the ideas of both the *domination of nature* and the *scientific method* took root in Western Europe. There is now a major thrust to deconstruct the Newtonian world outlook that collapsed scientific research with the so-called scientific method.

In a period when there is a better understanding of the multiple sources of knowledge there are numerous scholars who are clear that no society or people have a monopoly on scientific inquiry. Susantha Goonatilake has argued that the history of science is multi-cultural and the product of a dialogue among civilizations.[18] Studies on the *Racial Economy of Science* [19] and other interventions by third world scholars are seeking to repair the tremendous damage done to the world by the mechanical worldview that emanated from Western Europe. These studies have pointed to the cross fertilization of ideas between different societies over many centuries. This has led to Fritjof Kapra being explicit in the elaboration of the *Turning Point.*[20]

African scientists and the scientists of the world before the industrial revolution did not separate the material world from the spiritual world. The notion of an organic, living spiritual universe was the outlook of the majority of humanity before the impulse of *Capitalism and Slavery* in the forms of the industrial revolution represented world and the universe as a machine. The science of the era of western capitalism was based on a new method of inquiry advocated by Francis Bacon. Bacon advanced a mathematical description of nature. The analytical method of reasoning was given further credibility by Renee Descartes who asserted, 'I think therefore I am.' (Only men could think). Descartes stressed a sharp division between mind and body. The rational European males stressed the distinction between the observer and the observed. Europeans carried out witch hunting crusades and a philosophical outlook that denigrated women, privileged observation over reflection, matter over spirit and formulated a world view that was to dominate scientific thought for two or three centuries. Scientists detached themselves from the data, just as they isolated the data from the surrounding environment. Detached observation became the new criteria for objectivity. In the Twentieth Century many scientists sought to make a break with the Newtonian traditions and among the most notable was the eminent physicist, Albert Einstein.

Einstein had broken with *Nazi Science* in Germany and sought to make a fundamental break with any scientific tradition that celebrated a hierarchy of human beings. The theory of relativity was not only a contribution in scientific thought but Einstein was also a passionate defender of peace. Hence in the aftermath of splitting of the atom, Einstein worked hard to establish international institutions to ban the proliferation of nuclear weapons.

The laws and principles advanced by Isaac Newton had become known as the scientific revolution. Interwoven with concepts of predictability and determinism, nature as one machine, the market, Darwin's reductionist biology and Freud's concept of sex and sexuality, there was the formulation of a consistent body of thought that one calls the *European ideation system*.[21] In this ideation system there was a strict separation of mind, the body and the spirit. Spirituality could only be realized through a supreme male being so that the religious ideas of western Christianity were reformulated to be consistent with the mechanical ideas of the scientific revolution. Alienation from nature, the ideas of the domination over nature along with the religion that sanctified unlimited accumulation of wealth created a new phase in human history. The separation between mind and body, and between humans and nature with the idea that humans can dominate nature led to the generalized view that humans (especially non whites, women and nature) were fair game for domination. Indeed, in this mode of thinking domination and genocide were necessary components of progress. Progress was rational while it was in the best interest of humanity to dominate the irrational and feeble minded. According to the rational thinkers, Africans were not rational and were not fully human beings. No less a person than Frederich Hegel propagated the view that Africans were irrational and outside of history.

It was this ideation system that influenced those Africans that were educated in the institutions of higher learning in the imperial societies.[22] These social forces accepted the prevailing concepts of the academy as to who is developed, who is a full human and the purpose and the meaning of life. In this sense, the educated strata in the formal struggles for independence incorporated the very same set of European ideas that had been unleashed to justify the plunder of Africa.[23]

The acceptance of conquest, murder and plunder in the name of progress became a central feature of the European ideation system and the educated African internalized this concept of progress. Genocide and genocidal violence were considered legitimate in the name of nation building and 'security.' In the last decade of the twentieth century the fastest genocide in recent history took place with the Organization of African Unity paralyzed by the history of tolerance for military dictators and those who carried out genocide. The United Nations withdrew its small contingent at the height of the genocide.[24] This act in itself reflected the ways in which Africans had been written out of the genocide discourse.

The genocide in Central Africa, generalized violence, militarism and warfare, the spread of the AIDS pandemic,[25] along with the present debates on the politics of reproduction, bring alive the discussion on liberation and moves the debate away from the celebration of great leaders and the capture of state power. While the history of the ideas, forms of organization and leaders of liberation movements of the twentieth century are important, the youth and women who were not brought up in the era of anti-colonial struggles are bringing new questions to the challenge of liberation and liberation support. For many of the youths, the concepts of liberation that are now being promoted by Pan-African leaders do not touch the key issues of their lives: mis-education, unemployment, prison, alienation, glorification of violence and the mobilization of youths to fight (either in massive wars or against other members of their communities).

The mobilization and utilization of the African youth as child soldiers to defend patriarchs and masculinists who present themselves as liberators demand new forms of solidarity from Africans abroad. The particular experience of Sierra Leone should be of interest in so far as the Revolutionary United Front informed the Sierra Leonean people that they gained their inspiration from Bob Marley and the Rastafari movement in the Caribbean. There is an urgent requirement that Pan-African Organizations in the Caribbean be abreast of the latest information on the struggles against warfare in Africa so that there are no organizations that support dictators and repressive regimes in the name of Pan-Africanism. Pan-Africanists everywhere should critically examine the example of Laurent Kabila in his exhortation of Congolese citizens to go out and commit genocide in 1998.

Hiding behind tradition, while supporting violation and terror, has been a trademark of leaders who bought the most up to date instruments of death. Regional wars and military entrepreneurs reinforced the violence and structural economic conditions of exploitation that feminists and activists call *structural violence.* Throughout the continent, from the Cape to Cairo, African women have been at the forefront of stressing the truth that economic warfare and terrorism are reinforced by actual wars, sexual and gender violence, environmental degradation, psychological warfare and bio terrorism. The interconnections between sexual violence, militarism, masculinity, ideological illnesses, terrorism, economic exploitation, and information warfare form a feedback loop that is characteristic of the articulation of warfare.[26]

It is this articulation of the varying components of insecurity that is elusive precisely because of the binary categories that are employed in the analysis of liberation and peace. The concept of peace had been predicated on simply silencing guns and signing peace accords between warring elements. This concept of peace is based on 'managing chaos,' or the 'conflict resolution' paradigm. The challenge of the search for peace is to be able to link peace to a philosophy of life that celebrates humans as spiritual beings who do not separate thinking from feeling, compassion from observation, and spirit from matter. Pan-African liberation in this century is tied to spiritual renewal; how to transform social relations, family forms, concepts of community, city and economy, work and social reproduction.

The challenges of spiritual renewal become urgent in so far as at every stage of the social stirrings of the African masses reshaped the discourse on Pan-Africanism. Pan-Africanist leaders who internalized the ideas of progress, the scientific method and rationality, carried forward the idea that educated Africans would lead the masses out of poverty, ignorance and disease. It was this outlook that is usually termed Pan-Africanism of the elite or Pan-Africanism from above. During the period of segregation, colonialism and racism, the elite suffered from the discrimination and violence of the system. Hence, this elite found common cause with the poor. However, the elite wanted political power without fundamental political changes.

How can Africans be validated as human beings and lay the foundations for a new sense of personhood? This question has been sharpened by the major turning point in human transformations with the revolutionary technological changes that carried potential for healing as well as the potential for destruction. The questions of the worth of the value of African life, of human life will be contested in the 21st century.

Leaderism and the lessons of the Pan-African struggles in the last century

African-Americans, Caribbean people and movements and African descendants in Europe and other parts of the world have always been at the heart of Pan-African thought and action. This point has been articulated by many of the leading scholars on Pan-Africanism.[27] The violent separation and the oppression of the trans Atlantic slave trade lent urgency for identification with Africa. There is an important body of Pan -African thought that has argued that the idea of Pan-Africanism emanated from the enslaved person who wanted to develop a larger conception of reality than the village and the clan from which he or she was taken into captivity. The Atlantic slave trade captured the bodies of the Africans but could not capture their minds. Philosophically, ontologically and cosmologically, these captured humans never accepted the dehumanization of the system and the search for dignity emanated from this anti-slavery struggle. It is the memory of the courage of the fight of these people that continue to inspire the present struggles against modern slavery. But from that period of the Pan African revolts, there were those who accepted the philosophy and ideation system of the masters and those who completely resisted. There were also those who were schizophrenic and were torn between the culture and ideas of the oppressor and the ideas of the oppressed.

It is now possible to reflect on the meetings and resolutions of the seven Pan-African Congresses of the last century to assess the impact of the European ideation system on the Pan-African movement. [28] The immediate impetus for the first Pan- African Congress in 1900 was the barbarity of the pacification and partitioning of Africa. This conflict between Europeans in Africa had been partially resolved by the Congress of Berlin 1884-1885.[29] However, the partitioning did not end the constant wars of 'pacification,' that claimed the lives of millions. European colonizers carried out genocide in Africa with impunity and declared that this was done in the name of civilization.

The seven Congresses that were held from 1900 to 1994 were always being called to respond to the latest outrage by the imperialists. Usually, in the record of Pan Africanism in written literature, there is a great deal of emphasis on the Congresses but there were numerous manifestations of Pan-African solidarity and cooperation in the face of oppression, colonialism and apartheid. It was a major coincidence of history that the closing session of the 7th Pan-African Congress in Kampala, in April 1994, took place at the start of the fastest genocide in the Twentieth Century, the massacre of more than 800,000 Rwandans. The crimes of genocide carried out in the twentieth century have been many, with the decimation of the Congolese and the Namibians among the first. Usually, in the literature on genocide the killing of over one million Armenians by the Turks in 1916 is held as the first major genocide in this century. However, it was the industrial efficiency of the German military machine that brought the crime of genocide squarely before the attention of humanity.

Germany had rehearsed this genocide in Namibia before perfecting gas chambers and death camps that consumed more than 24,000 daily. The genocide of the fascists against Jews, homosexuals, Roma Peoples (called gypsies), Poles, communists and others, created internationally the awareness of the nature of genocide. Auschwitz, the name of one of the more notorious death camps in Poland, became synonymous with mass extermination. It was the reality of this holocaust that created the slogan; "Never Again," to register that humanity would never again tolerate genocide. However, in the aftermath of the experience of the genocide in Rwanda (and other parts of Africa) and the international response, it is not clear whether the idea of genocide is reserved for only one section of humanity.

Adam Hochschild in the book, *King Leopold's Ghost* brought out the fact of the more than ten million Africans that were massacred in the Congo by the agents and functionaries of the Belgian monarch, King Leopold. This study draws heavily from the work of African-Americans who in the 19th century were in the forefront of opposing this genocide. Forty years ago, Malcolm X brought up the genocide of the Belgians but the University professors dismissed the claim to say that this was an exaggeration. The kind of Pan-African solidarity that was represented by African American missionaries in the Congo is very different from those who cover up imperial plunder by fundamentalists who use various disguises to penetrate the African country side. The legacies of wanton destruction of African lives continue today in Burundi, Eastern Congo, Rwanda and other parts of Central Africa. Pan-Africanists must continue to oppose genocide and make the slogan *Never Again* a reality for all humans.

Throughout the Twentieth Century, the vibrant identification with Africa among African-Americans and the Caribbean peoples was linked to the struggles against colonialism, racism and segregation in the African Diaspora. From the period of the Italian invasion of Abyssinia in

1935, through the struggles against fascism and genocide, Africans engaged in movements to advance the cause of freedom. The literature on liberation and liberation support has drawn attention to the deep traditions of solidarity work with Africa. Studies on the History of Pan-African Revolts brought to life the black radical traditions of the beginning of the century as well as the leaders of these movements.[30] These scholarly works have augmented the movements but the major limitation of this literature was the emphasis on great leaders. Individuals such as Marcus Garvey or Malcolm X were famous Pan-African thinkers and leaders but it is important that the study and understanding of Pan-Africanism do not minimize the important role of the millions of ordinary men and women who inspired and supported these individuals. This is the principal argument of African women who are calling for the engendering of Pan Africanism.[31]

Despite the limitations of Pan-Africanism from above and the Pan-Africanism of great males, the global Pan-African movement has historically been one of the principal currents of political change and a force against racism on both sides of the Atlantic. In the twentieth century the great Pan-African leaders, George Padmore, Marcus Garvey, C.L.R. James, W.E.B. Du Bois, Malcolm X. Walter Rodney and countless of others accepted the challenge of rolling back the frontiers of colonialism in Africa and the Caribbean and segregation in the USA. The definition of Pan-Africanism at that moment assumed that the content and meaning of political independence would advance the dignity of the African. Kwame Nkrumah, who had urged, 'Seek Ye the Political Kingdom and all will be added to thee,' had underlined this position. A stratum that had internalized certain concepts of politics, state, government and people undertook the organizational task for this brand of Pan-Africanism.

It is now possible to critically examine and assess the

concept of the 'political kingdom.' Stress should also be placed on the fact that the end of colonialism did not come from the gift of the colonizers or from the activities of leaders. Colonialism ended because of the agency, because of the sacrifices of the people. As Walter Rodney observed, 'one must go back to this underlying movement of history and have confidence in the capacity of our people: if they could have breached the gates of colonialism through their own effort, then it seems to me that they have brought into the neo-colonial period a capacity to breach the walls of imperialism.[32]

There is a narrative in South Africa where the effort is to deny the major sacrifices of the youth and to write of the end of apartheid as a miracle of negotiations between F.W. De Klerk and Nelson Mandela. [33] The victory of the global anti-apartheid movement in 1994 was a major turning point in the last century. The concentration on the negotiations of great men has been part of the tradition of western scholarship in every case in Africa. Both Sembene Ousmane and Ngugi Wa Thiongo have sought in literary works to bring to the fore the struggles of the ordinary men and women in the independence struggles. The role of women in the struggles for independence has not been properly documented. There is the sterling example of the *Symbolism of the Nigerian Women's War of 1929*: and every society in Africa had major anti-colonial interventions by women.[34]

From the inception of the OAU in 1963 there are those leaders who wanted to institutionalize a form of Pan-Africanism that excluded the majority of the producers: the ordinary workers, peasants, traders, religious leaders, business persons and cultural artists. This has reached a point where one has to be self critical when using the formulation of Pan-Africanism. This is because the social and economic conditions among African peoples have reached the point where, instead of liberation and self determination, super exploitation and alienation prevail. Consequently, instead of the liberation stories serving as a source of inspiration to the youth to bring about better living conditions in the future, the present process is seen as a never ending nightmare of destruction, death, unemployment and greed.

Many of the leaders of the past Pan-African movement and the liberation struggles have contributed to this sense of nightmare. This need to expose criminal African leaders (whether they be Charles Taylor or Foday Sankoh) continues to be important, so that those who are calling for reparations cannot be disarmed by alliances with leaders and demagogues who will take just causes to repair injustice and make them illegitimate causes. President Robert Mugabe of Zimbabwe is an excellent example of a leader who was once at the forefront of the liberation struggle, but whose tenure of office did not assist the project of bettering the lives of the people. This is an example of a leader who has devalued a just cause of the need to repair the injustice associated with the settler seizure of land during colonialism. The land question is very emotional for Africans all over the world. There is a struggle for land and for the rights of working peoples in all parts of the Caribbean. It is for this reason that in the support of the struggles for land it is crucial that there is the support of the principle of the return of the land to the Zimbabwean peoples, especially the farm workers and the rural women in the communal sector. By resorting to the same violence and force of the colonizers without using other legal and political instruments available for the redistribution of land to the tillers, the political leadership weakened and postponed the process of national reconstruction.

This author believes that it is up to Africans to take the lead to oppose the brutality meted out against Zimbabweans while rejecting the moral claims of Europe of passing sanctions against Zimbabweans. The late Julius Nyerere of Tanzania demonstrated the practicality of opposing an

African dictator (Idi Amin), while ensuring that the West did not claim the moral high ground for the opposition to Amin. Similarly, in this period, Zimbabwean women, who have felt the brunt of gender violence and the politics of intolerance, gender violence, rape and the denial of full rights of citizenship are making a call for the opposition of the Zimbabwe government that is quite different from the opposition of the British and US governments.

The Pan-African movement has to be self-critical because early, when there were massacres in Matebeleland (in Zimbabwe), the Pan-Africanists were quiet. Then, there was the persecution of women as prostitutes. Pan-Africanists were again silent. This silence persisted in the face of the manipulation of the land issue, the rush to integrate into the colonial army, the persecution of the workers and those of a different sexual orientation. These silences emboldened the leadership of Zimbabwe to proclaim themselves as the leaders of the Pan African forces for liberation. Concretely, this proclamation took the form of support for the Kabila government in the Democratic Republic of the Congo and the training of the Interahamwe, those who had committed genocide in Rwanda. This government has demonstrated concretely the example of the dead end of Pan-Africanism from above. Leaders such as those in Zimbabwe can be found all over the continent and it is from these experiences that the Pan-African movement must take the responsibility to disassociate itself from Pan-Africanism from above or what is called the patriarchal model of liberation.

Movements in struggle and parties in government began to clarify very early the difference between Pan-Africanism of the elite, or Pan-Africanism of those with state power and Pan-Africanism from below. From the beginning of the last century, some of the leaders started to think of stepping into the shoes of the colonialists. Some of the most articulate spokespersons of the Pan-African/Negritude movement reneged on one of the cardinal principles of Pan-Africanism that 'the people of one part of Africa are responsible for the freedom and liberation of their brothers and sisters in other parts of Africa and indeed black people everywhere were to accept the same responsibility.[35]

Throughout the Caribbean there were Pan-Africanists who supported African liberation but did not support the struggles for peace and democracy in Haiti. It is imperative that the just struggles of the peoples of Haiti and Cuba are supported. The peoples of the Caribbean must continue to demonstrate their solidarity with the Cuban Revolution. It is not widely known by the current generation the sacrifices that were made by the Cuban people for the African Liberation struggle. More significantly, progressive persons in the Caribbean must continue to discuss and clarify the nature of the forms of political intervention that led to the defeat of the Grenadian Revolution. The Grenadian experience demonstrated the full consequences of the politics of intolerance where political leaders were not able to solve political differences through non-violent means.

The recourse to violence continues to be a major problem in this period. The leaders instead foment the ideological diseases that placed the African continent in war and violence. These wars emanate from the principal ideological illnesses of the period and liberation will not be possible until we identify and seek to heal from these illnesses. The four main ideological illnesses are Ethnicism (tribalism), religious intolerance (witnessed all over the African world inside and outside of Africa), fetishism, and male chauvinism. The social composition of the OAU, along with the inability to intervene to promote peace has demonstrated the limits of male centered politics. The African women are organizing and are demanding an end to gender violence. These women and peace activists have forced the issue of liberation and peace in Africa on the agenda.

Retreating from wars and violence

African women have become the pre-eminent force for peace and have made it clear that peace is one of the most important goals of Pan-Africanism in this century.[36] All over Africa there have been wars and conflict to the point where the writings on Africa suggest that warfare is endemic to Africa. The existence of wars all across the African continent (in Angola, Burundi, the Congo Republic, Democratic Republic of the Congo, Eritrea, Ethiopia, Rwanda, Somalia, Sudan, Uganda and parts of Nigeria) demands explanations beyond the simplistic notions of warlordism or the criminalization of the state in Africa. It is becoming fashionable to view 'tribal Africa' as being in a Hobbesian state of war. At the very seat of the OAU (in Ethiopia) where there should be the example of peaceful resolution of conflicts, instead there is a senseless war.

In Eritrea and Ethiopia militarists resorted to 19th century technology to kill and maim over borders. This was an obvious example of the devaluation of the lives of Africans. There are numerous other examples in the Sudan, Liberia, Sierra Leone, Central Africa, Angola and the Great Lakes where the reasons for war have now become very remote. Whatever may have been the reasons for the start of the war in the Congo it is now clear that only the Lusaka Agreement provides an opportunity to move from this senseless war. From the point of view of the arms merchants and diamond dealers the wars make good business sense in a world ruled by the God of Profit. However, for ordinary mortals that value life over profit these wars make no sense. The business of warfare is compounded by the low respect for human life. This low respect for human life has led different leaders to think that armed confrontation is necessarily superior to social transformations through democratic, peaceful, and persuasive and community based political interventions. It is the respect for human life that is at the base of the call for the reconceptualization of Pan-Africanism. The short-term tasks of transforming the colonial legacy of disrespect for human life is tied to the medium term and long term tasks of transforming the whole economic basis of society.

The written call of respect for human life is not new but was started by David Walker of the USA way back in the 19th century when in his appeal he defined the tasks of Pan-Africanism as

> the full glory and happiness, as well as that of all other colored people under heaven, shall never be consummated without the entire emancipation of your enslaved brethren all over the world.[37]

This was the essence of Pan-Africanism from below, the emancipation of peoples all over the world and not simply the acquisition of political power.

The call for the global redefinition of Pan-Africanism has been carried out by every generation since David Walker. This reappraisal is continuing, but unfortunately the movement has so far responded to the written words and not to the oral traditions of Pan-Africanism. In privileging the written word, the voices of women have been silenced in the definition of Pan-Africanism.

African women and liberation

Many African women have been critical of the male centered concepts of Pan-Africanism. Many of the intellectuals who have written on Pan-Africanism have formulated and reconstructed Pan-Africanism as a male enterprise.

There are numerous examples on the oppression of African women and the silence of Pan-Africanists inside and outside of Africa. Whatever the forms of sexual and gender violence, the violation of women has been one of the foremost manifestations of oppression in Africa. African women who are struggling against oppression continue to call for a new focus on liberation. In the past year, the case of Safiya Hussein gripped the attention of the women's movement and Progressive Pan Africanists. In Nigeria, Safiya Hussein was sentenced to death by stoning by a Sharia court in the Northwestern state of Sokoto. She was convicted of 'adultery' in 2001, but her sentence was deferred because she was pregnant. She was supposed to be put to death but the case had provoked revulsion, anger and mobilization by women all over the world, especially African women. The same court that found Safiya guilty of adultery set the male partner free on the grounds that there were no witnesses. The laws in the Sharia courts are gender biased to the extreme. These extremes are manifestations of the gender discrimination that African women face in every sphere of activity.

In modern societies, gender differences serve as the most basic source of inequality and this has been major weakness of the Pan-African movement and hence the stalemate in moving forward. Simply 'adding women' to organizations and having them in positions will not change the conditions of women. Recently, the female parliamentarians of South Africa realized that with women pressing for transparency in Parliament, the discussions of the budget and decisions on military matters were taken out of the parliament into specialized technical committees. It is clearer, after thirty years of the organizing of African women, that confronting the problems of male chauvinism and gender violence cannot be dealt with through affirmative action alone. What it demands for rectification is a radical restructuring of thought and analysis which once and for all accepts the fact that humanity consists in equal parts of men and women and that the experiences, thoughts, and insights of both sexes must be represented in every generalization that is made about human beings.

This call from the feminist movement for the restructuring of thought and analysis is also necessary for the Pan-African movement. The contribution of feminists in general and African feminists in particular is forcing all scholars to rethink the ideas of the most progressive who spoke of the rights of man or the new man. Nearly all of the nationalist leaders in Africa, even the most progressive fell into the trap of speaking for men as if this represented all of the population. The limitation is being addressed by those who seek to extend the numbers of women in politics but this problem cannot be rectified by adding women, it requires a fundamental rethinking of the categories of gender, politics and the state.

From Egypt to South Africa and from Brazil to Bermuda African women are redefining the issues of peace, politics and responsibility. The struggle of Nawa El Sadawi in Egypt over her rights as a woman is replicated all over the continent of Africa where men seek to own the bodies and minds of women. Women are demanding their rights as citizens and in the process of defending their rights to integrity and personhood are exposing decisions such as that relating to Safiya Hussein. The experiences of Safiya Hussein exposed the last ditch efforts of African patriarchs to place women in spaces where they can be dominated and controlled. At the present moment Pan-African activists are being held to a higher standard so that within the Pan-African movement there is no tolerance of gender violence. At the 1994 Southern African Regional Conference to prepare for the seventh Pan- African Congress, it was resolved that no person can hold office in the Pan-African movement or hold any office if that person engages in domestic violence. This is a principle that all Pan-African organizations are encouraged to accept.

The story is told of one of the major leaders of the Pan-African movement who left his children in the orphanage. The children wrote a book entitled: *In Search of Mr. McKenzie.* The point was to underline that one cannot be political and revolutionary on the platform and be a despot at home.

In the Pan-African movement, women and youth have begun to challenge the long-standing assumptions in the discussions of Pan-Africanism. The assumptions of knowledge, politics, and social change are therefore undergoing great changes. [38] This emerged quite clearly from the 1999 Pan-African Women's Conference on peace in Zanzibar. The declaration on Peace was most far-reaching and challenged males to rethink old ideas of 'managing conflicts.'

 Eusi Kwayana one of the contemporary activists of the movement took up the challenge and stated in his call to African males that:

> The cultural constitution of Africa in relation to women and in relation to youth is in need of revision. And this cannot be done behind the backs of the youth and the women. Pan-Africanism will have validity only when it seeks to solve the fundamental problems of social injustice among Africans and supports every human community in its efforts for justice, freedom and development.[39]

However, African women are calling for more than support from African males. Patricia Mc Fadden called for men to make a conceptual and political leap in supporting women's struggles. She argued that:

> In order to make the conceptual and political leap from supporting women's struggles for freedom, to initiating a process of freeing themselves from patriarchal backwardness, black men will have to

understand not only the necessity of interrogating male privilege as it relates to them as men, but they will also have to locate that understanding at the intersection of race, class, age and social status as all these issues affect their identities and their relationship with power. They will need to understand and accept, for example, that while being against gender violence has now become the politically correct stance to adopt, because women have fought uncompromising battles to wrestle the issue of impunity from the domestic arena by making it a crime to violate a woman in any way and place in most societies in the world (although the issue of marital rape remains intractable and outstanding in this sense), it is not politically correct to continue to hold on to the ancient, undemocratic practice of violating children whether this takes the form of sexual violence (which is still justified by certain cultural claims in some African societies), or physical and psychological violence, supposedly for purposes of discipline.[40]

Reconceptualizing Pan-Africanism

The statement of McFadden on impunity and Kwayana's invitation to rethink the cultural constitution in relation to women are simple and straightforward and help us to define Pan-African liberation in the 21st century. It is this challenge that forces the necessity to reassess how to define Pan-Africanism.

In 1974 at the time of the sixth Pan-African Congress in Tanzania, Walter Rodney wrote that, Pan-Africanism is an exercise in self definition which is undertaken by a specific social group or social class which speaks on behalf of the population as a whole. Walter Rodney asked a number of salient questions: Which class was leading the national movement? How capable was this class in carrying out the tasks of national liberation? What are the silent classes on whose behalf the calls for Pan-African liberation were being made?

The answer to these questions has been made easier by the experiences of the Pan- African leaders all over the world. The assumption of power by black leaders in Africa, black mayors in the USA, leaders of government in the Caribbean, black parliamentary representatives in Europe has not changed the conditions of existence of the majority. If anything, in the era of globalization the exploitation of the masses of the people has intensified. This exploitation is being carried out under the neo-liberal ideas of liberalization that redistributes wealth from the exploited to the powerful. The fact that the Pan-African leadership of yesterday now constitutes the problem and the obstacles to emancipation helps us to sharpen the conception of Pan-Africanism from below.

Bonita Harris and the Red Thread movement in Guyana have been critical of the actions and politics of even radical males in 'Pan-African organizations.' African women have not accepted Pan-Africanism from above since they viewed the self-definition in relation to Europeans. African women from the grassroots are at the forefront of developing a new self-definition of the movement. At the 7th Pan- African Congress in Uganda 1994 the women who were gathered there formed the Pan-African Women Liberation Organization. African women are calling for freedom from all forms of oppression. There is the representation that the struggle against patriarchy, sexism, homophobia and racism are now different parts of the same struggle for dignity.

The question that Rodney posed in relation to self-definition was which class was leading the self-definition.

Kwayana of Guyana argued that Pan-Africanism should be understood:

> as a body of thought and action shared but not uniform or dogmatic. A dynamic movement continuing transforming itself and gaining new ideological perspectives in light of changing circumstance. Flowing from masses, groups and occasionally leaders of governments. Tending to the goal of the restoration of freedom and dignity at home and abroad.[41]

Kwayana continued:

> Pan-Africanist thought and action must seek to establish in these impatient and righteously restless times the fact that Africa was a source of civilization and culture of the highest order; that Africans will no longer stand at the end or near the end of the lowest queue in the world; that Africans must empower themselves by themselves or jointly with groups willing to share power, in and out of Africa, to overcome the social and economic evils of the day to promote human development; that oppression of Africans by Africans must not be tolerated; that there must be an international African jury to consider the human wastage in Angola, Rwanda and in any other divided African country to resolve the situation; that in addition to the traditional respect for elders we should raise up a new tradition, respect for young people also; that Africans must lead the world in the use of all means to assist African women and girls (and all women) to their rightful place in the family and in society.[42]

Pan-Africanism according to Kwayana must grasp

representations of Pan-Africanism in the streets, in the communities, in the villages and in the voices of those who aspire for freedom, dignity and humanity.

Pan-African renewal in the 21st century

Two key concepts are relevant for the discussion on renewal. The first is with respect to the rehabilitation of the human spirit and the second is with respect to the humanization of the planet. In the first place, the Pan-African struggle involves a major assault on the instrumental and capitalistic values associated with the idea of the domination of nature and the second is in relation to who could be masters and possessors of nature. Europeans (especially males) were rational human beings who through biological inheritance of intellectual distinction were through a process of natural selection superior to Africans. Africans were naturally inferior because they had been unable to master nature. Their views on totemage, on the respect for nature and for respecting the immensity of the universe were dismissed as primitive superstition. In the discussion of Pan-Africanism from above, there was never a serious discussion on totems and the Pan-African unity inspired by totems.

Malidoma Some in his book on the *Healing Wisdom of Africa* reinforced the ideas that in most societies, including Africa, humans were part of nature and had a material and spiritual base in the Universe. The forests were the reservoir of medicine and the animals represented part of the ancestry of humans. In the Western European ideation system, humans were like machines without a spiritual core and the rational individual made choices that maximized life circumstances. John Locke, the English philosopher developed the idea of the rational self-interested individual with property in their bodies. John Locke's theory of property played a critical role in shaping the intellectual traditions of the West with respect to individualism. It is this theory of rationality that is at the centre of the ideas of the WTO with respect to intellectual property rights.

Africans and the patenting of life forms. Is life an invention?

The present opposition to the food and pharmaceuticals companies represents one of the most important aspects of the struggles for liberation. These companies are deciding on who can control the life giving resources of the planet earth. The fundamental issue for all peoples is that of the patenting of life forms. This is of tremendous importance to all peoples. Peoples of African descent in the Caribbean and Central America must link up with African organizations that are part of the South–South network to defend local knowledge and local genetic materials. Throughout Central and South America there is a renewed effort to expropriate crucial resources that have been protected by the African and indigenous peoples. The same companies that are carrying out bioprospecting in the Caribbean are also involved in the new scramble for genetic resources in Africa.

Given that two countries in Africa hold the greatest quantity and quality of resource base in diverse genetic animal and plant materials, there is a greater awareness by those in the Africa knowledge network that genetic materials represent a globally strategic resource that, if properly developed, could be the basis of real qualitative leaps in reconceptualizing economics in this century.

In the past three years since WTO meetings in Seattle of 1999, the technical work by African based NGOs demonstrated a number of concrete lessons for all Africans. The first and most important was the ability to stand up for the rights of Africans and to be technically prepared at international negotiating sessions. The second important lesson was the impact of the solidarity of other former colonized peoples from India, China, Brazil, Malaysia and other Third World societies in shaping international questions.

Up to now (May 2002) despite many efforts to divide Africans with discussions of partnerships, the Africa group at the international trade negotiations successfully rejected the efforts and pressures used by developed nations to divide African nations. The cooperation at the meetings of the WTO represents another example of the potential global strength of Pan Africanism as a framework for building conceptualizations of Africa's global interests, even when interests of individual nations don't coincide. The fact that the Third World is lined up behind the Africa Group's position paper on Trade Related Intellectual Property Rights (TRIPs), means that Africa will have a major say in global rules covering intellectual property rights, and protecting the interests of peasants, farmers, and future generations world-wide to retain local control over indigenous knowledge and universal human access to what nature provides for all of humanity.

A similar cooperation was exhibited by the African Descendants Caucus in the meetings of the World Conference against Racism. It is the view of this author, that the efforts to develop NEPAD without the people, is an attempt by the G7 to break the renewed solidarity of Africans that was demonstrated at the WTO meetings (in Seattle in 1999) and at the World Conference against Racism (Durban 2001). The fact that African NGOs were able to work with, and monitor the actions of African government officials (checks and balances) to represent and protect the interests of African peoples in a global platform was a clear expression of the possible directions of the present Pan-African movement. These are principles that all the peoples of Africa will find valuable in their own process that are related to *emancipatory politics*.

The Africa group, African descendants and all oppressed peoples will have to continue to work against those interests which benefit from the continued plunder of the globe and who support the neo liberal principles that enrich a few. Organic Pan-African intellectuals will need to continue to expose the inequality in the nature of world trade. They will especially have to expose the development and exploitation of the natural resources of Africa via the exclusion of Africa's human resources and separate from the colonial and World Bank economic frameworks. This task is linked to the expansion of the reparations debate to cover all areas of restitution.

The tasks of the corporations at the present are how to defeat the ideas of emancipatory politics, how to defeat ideas of a planetary cooperation and social collectivism and concepts of security that elaborate the humanity of human beings everywhere. This is urgent in the era of the emergence of eugenic thinking. Eugenics is based on the idea that there are superior and inferior breeds of the human species. The idea of the eugenic civilization is one of the key aspects of the present biotech revolution.

The *Bio Tech Century*

In the book *Biotech Century*, Jeremy Rifkin identifies seven components of what he calls the new operational matrix for the biotech century we have just entered. The first is the ability of scientists to isolate and recombine the genetic make up of humans, plants and animals. A handful of global corporations, research institutions and governments seek to hold patents on all 100,000 genes that make up the blue print of the human race, as well as the cells, organs and tissues that comprise the human body.

The second component is that of a newly defined incentive given out to those in the field of biotechnology who discover and create genetic material of all sorts.

The third component is that of the 'Second Genesis' where biotechnology and pharmaceutical companies will have the power and the ability to fertilize the earth with a new generation of genetically modified and non naturally occurring seeds, plants, animals and ecosystems.

The fourth component is that of the creation of a newly defined eugenic society. This component that involves the whole ethics of cloning provides the basis for a new form of biological engineering that is based on the hierarchy of humans.

The fifth component is the scientific move away from the role of the environment in shaping humans (nurture) towards the role of biology and genetic composition (nature).

The sixth component is the marriage of the computer and the biotech culture in order to manipulate, interpret, and manage the extent of genetic discoveries.

The seventh component is the change in the cosmological view of the world. What is natural and what is nature is being reformulated by a handful of scientists in the pay of giant companies.

Rifkin noted that:

> The marriage of computers and genes forever alters our reality at the deepest level of the human experience. To begin to comprehend the enormity of the shift taking place in human civilization, it is important to step back and gain a better understanding of the historic nature of the many changes that are occurring all around us as we turn the corner into a new century. We are in the throes of one of the great transformations in world history.[43]

The revolutionary scientific advances in biotechnology

are redefining the meaning of life, liberty and equality. The great transformations in the world pose great opportunities and challenges for the African liberation experience. One of the great challenges will be in the area of the normalization of the idea of eugenics and the power of the rich to decide on who has the right to live. Eugenics and biotechnology merge in the context of those companies that want to have complete control over African resources.

At any moment in the history of capitalism it is imperative to grasp the leading edge of accumulation and to see how these forces shape the policies of governments. In the period of monopoly capitalism, the search for minerals had propelled companies in the wake of the technological changes that ushered in fordism. The breakthroughs in molecular biology and genetic engineering place biotech companies on par with the other leading elements in cybernetics and telecommunications. Africa's biodiverse environment is now the primary target of the international capitalists. Africa is the home to some of the world's most endemic floral and faunal species. Two of the globe's megadiversity sites are located in Southern Africa. This region had endured centuries of colonial conservation and accumulation schemes divorced from the interests of the African peoples.

As the biotech revolution and the research in genetic engineering accelerate, the polarization in the world between the rich and powerful and the downtrodden and exploited will be magnified. There is at present, bioprospecting in Africa for genetic resources with the pressures to harvest the genetic resources in a way that would alienate African communities from the very forms of life they depended for their survival. The interventions by external forces not only created harmful effects on African communities, but also introduced uniform methods of handling biodiversity. In Southern Africa, the Africans not only lost their land but the right to seeds. It is this generalized form of expropriation that is projected in the Twenty First Century. The United States agribusiness interests have already started deploying resources in Africa to lay the building blocks for the forms of agricultural production and marketing of the next fifty years.

Today, the Earth's atmosphere and life-sustaining resources are being altered by international capital as never before. *Biopiracy: the Plunder of Humans and Nature* is being driven by the consumption patterns of the West (manifest most obscenely in the extensive burning of fossil fuels), clearing of tropical forests, and other changes in the use of natural and agricultural landscapes.[44] After centuries of attempting to break collective ownership of land and plant life in Africa, there is now a major push to erode all vestiges of collective ownership. In Africa, the availability of diverse natural life forms has for time immemorial been integral to human existence. Everyday Africans conceive of biodiversity in social and spiritual frames that encompass an organic way in which their communities sustain and reproduce themselves. Whether it is by traditional medicinal healing, or hunting, plants and animals provide the living ingredients for basic human continuity.

The intent of the WTO rules on Trade Related Intellectual Property Rights, is to criminalize Africans for harvesting plants and seeds in Africa in the ways in which this harvesting has gone on for centuries. Once the criminalization of African property rights is constructed in security terms, then the psychological operations of the West can influence the public to endorse military interventions on behalf of pharmaceuticals.

Biological diversity (the extraordinary variety of genes, species and habitats that comprise life on Earth) is being rapidly and irrevocably diminished as the consumption habits of humanity transform forests and other natural habitats to human uses deplete marine and aquaculture fisheries, and stress remaining natural habitats through pollution and atmospheric change. Human-made chemicals have damaged the stratospheric ozone layer that protects people, plants and animals from harmful ultraviolet radiation. These and other patterns of global environmental change are, in turn, driven by a combination of the unbridled commodity fetishism of the West, high consumption of energy and natural resources, and perverse market driven policy incentives.

There is an urgent need for a global movement and partnership against the biotech firms that are involved in genetic engineering solely for the benefit of the rich. Africans at home and abroad must be astute enough to join with the forces that are against globalization in all parts of the world. Western biotech companies threaten an enormous decline in the number of plant and animal species on earth. These companies are embarking on the production of genetically modified seeds and genetically modified foods that threaten to disrupt traditional checks and balances in nature. The new methods of handling biodiversity are geared towards servicing the needs of Western companies that treat African biodiversity as a global resource, thus allowing global firms full access to valuable genetic information. Past and present bio-prospecting activities for plant ingredients, which prove to be valuable for US and European pharmaceutical and bio-tech industries, do not address questions of compensation or cultural natural rights of Africans. For this reason, African states are at the forefront of the battle to amend the rules of the WTO with respect to the mandatory patenting of life forms. This collective thrust by Africa in alliance with countries such as India, Venezuela and Malaysia to amend the rules of the WTO is opposed by the United States.

USA and their concept of partnering with Africa

To disguise the plunder of African resources, the government of the USA presents itself as developing new partnership with Africa: The essence of the African Growth and Opportunity Act (AGOA) is to strengthen the relative position of US capitalists in relation to other global capitalists. This would place the US in the drivers' seat in order to ensure that the US would dominate access to the resources of Africa. African leaders are struggling over land, while the pharmaceutical companies are going into the villages to obtain the knowledge in the heads of the traditional healers and botanists. The US wants unlimited liberalization to have access to all of the genetic materials in Africa. This is the essence of the activism of the USA in relation to partnership with Africa as manifest in activities such as the AGAO legislation and the military partnership as envisaged in the Africa Crisis Response Initiative, later renamed Africa Contingency Operations Training Assistance (ACOTA).

There is such strong competition between the European Union and the USA over the resources of Africa, that the European Union has put forward their own Economic Partnership Agreement (EPA). The objective of the EPA between the EU and the African states is to ensure that Africa remains a market for European products and be a source of cheap raw materials and labor. The negotiations of the Partnership Agreements have not yet raised the issues of the crimes of Europe in Africa.

What the authors of the new partnerships in Europe and the USA do not address are the questions of the health, safety and well being of African societies, particularly the peasant sector that depend on plant life for food and medicine. It was significant that at the same time the US Legislation on AGOA was making its way through the legislative process, US pharmaceuticals were taking the South African government to court over its intention to manufacture low cost generic versions of high priced essential medicines patented western pharmaceuticals. The drugs that could turn AIDS from a death sentence into a chronic disease were available on the international market for over US $12,000. The prohibitively high cost of the drugs guaranteed, that in a region where the highest death rates in the world from AIDS were recorded, the majority of the people would not have access to the drugs. South Africa had passed an act in 1997 allowing the government to both manufacture the drugs and also to import such drugs cheaply. AIDS and the debilitating effects of this pandemic reflect the divide between the concern for life in Africa and the concern with profits by the USA.

In the face of the grassroots pressures from activist organizations such as the Treatment Action Campaign (TAC), the South African government successfully resisted the US government. This represents another example of resisting the imperial arrogance. There is the need for more coordinated Pan-African response to the AIDS pandemic. For millions of HIV infected persons, there is a crying need to make life saving drugs more available. Accelerating the preventive efforts require more transparency and leadership from governments and massive investments in public health systems, and making quality health care much more widely available. This in turn requires major new investments in public health and the abandonment of structural adjustment requirements to collect user fees from people seeking health care.

In this struggle, women are again at the forefront. The Women's movement across Africa is calling for all women to respond to the HIV/AIDS crisis by demanding 'legally guaranteed reproductive and sexual rights which must be linked to the provision of adequate and accessible health care services, information and the facilitation of choice in terms of sexual relationships, reproductive abilities and counseling.'[45] The AIDs pandemic more than any other factor demands a new agenda in international relations. This agenda is being shaped by the reparations debate.

Reparations and Peace In Africa

The concept of reparations has gained currency in the last century as the basis for restitution and redress for past crimes. The meaning of reparations under international law includes: (a) restitution, (b) compensation, (c) rehabilitation and (d) guarantee of non-recurrence. According to the definitions of reparations, there is payment or other compensation provided by a government to a group of people or to another country to compensate for loss or damage that it has caused. Internationally, reparations have been paid after a war by the losers to the winners, most notably by Germany after World War 1. The payments made to the state of Israel and to the victims of the German Holocaust have brought the question of reparations for crimes firmly on the international agenda.

Throughout Africa, the need for restitution and redress is manifest in all spheres of life and society. Ordinary men and women support the reparations demand and call for a new mode of economics. Those leaders who are seeking to reproduce Europe in Africa are retreating from the debate on reparations. These leaders seek compromises that downplay the history of crimes and genocide. In particular, African leaders who have put forward the NEPAD (sometimes called New African Initiative (NAI) have been willing to jettison the debate on reparations in deals that would lead to European investment in new plans for Western exploitation of labor and genetic resources. These leaders who have succumbed to the 'Washington Consensus' are outside of the discourse of those who want to ensure that the violations are never repeated.

There is a clear refusal on the part of the contemporary leadership who consider themselves to be civilized by Europeans to grasp the depth of the crimes committed. Hence, in a context such as the Democratic Republic of the Congo, where the record of the slave trade and genocide is compelling, the political leadership seeks deals that can perpetuate the models of exporting primary commodities inherited from King Leopold. The example of the crimes committed by Belgium in the massacre of more than ten million Africans has now been exposed and the old discourse of Belgian civilization has been exposed as a project of murder.[46] This tradition was sealed in the participation of the Belgian state in the brutal assassination of Patrice Lumumba and the war to defeat the independence struggle of the Congolese people.[47]

While the Belgian government has accepted moral responsibility for the assassination of Patrice Lumumba, there has been no effort to raise the issue of full disclosure of the truth of Belgian genocide as the prelude to a fundamental reconstruction program. In the specific case of Burundi, the government of Belgium has been most active to ensure that the people of Burundi do not spell out the implications of the assassination of Prince Rwagasora for the violent political history of Burundi. Belgium should be a test case for the African Union in demanding reparations, in so far as certain social forces in Belgium have aligned themselves in the campaign to try international war criminals. The experiences of the French and British crimes are so huge that the building of African unity will be tested in the exposure of these crimes. The struggle against exploitation and the road to peace is intertwined with the clearing of the record of the past and present racist crimes of Europe in Africa.

The war in Central Africa attests to these legacies of crimes, assassinations, xenophobia, intolerance and genocide. As the debate on reparations deepens in the solidarity across continents, there will be the representation of all the forces: those who want the monetary compensation, the return of cultural artifacts stolen from Africa, those who call for debt cancellation, those who support the European and US view that African chiefs participated and are just as culpable and those who want a clean change in the social system, in short those who are tabling the issue of *moral reparations*. The full mobilization of international political forces will be necessary to ensure that there is a full airing of the crimes.

It is within the collective consciousness of the producers that their sacrifices were forgotten as a small educated stratum sought to intensify colonial economic relations. This has meant that even in the contemporary period of the struggle to build the African Union, when there should be a clear demand for compensation from oil companies for their wanton destruction of the environment, governments would rather kill the activists calling for redress than confront the petroleum companies. Reference had already been made to the Mugabe experience where the land struggle was not over new relations on the land and the defense of African plants, water resources, seeds and knowledge, but, for the aspiring African elite to control and own the land once seized by whites. This example of the land struggles in Zimbabwe is an important component of the search for the values and qualities needed for *healing* and for peace.

The search for peace and for new qualities for leadership is informing the embryonic debate and contestations around reparations. On the African continent there are those leaders who have forgotten all of the principles of solidarity with those Africans who are dispersed across the globe and face day to day racist attacks in Europe. Leaders who are silent on the brutal murders of Africans in North America and the criminalization of the youth, enter into agreements with US military. These leaders do not understand that the issue of crimes against humanity and the nature of the criminal states that orchestrated these crimes cannot be negotiated.

While there are a number of lines of thought for peace, security and justice in the African Union, there is also the slow but clear awareness of some sections of the movement that reparations cannot be simply about financial compensation, but, must include redress for contemporary forms of violation and servitude and the search for new relations so that those who are compensated cannot be a force for strengthening the same relations and ideas that justified genocide. There are many examples of monetary compensation for victims of crimes against humanity in the last century, but, in many instances these payments were made to ensure the continuation of the present forms of global inequality and exploitation.

The example of the State of Israel and the relations with the peoples of Palestine exposed the reality that even those who suffered from genocide can become perpetrators of human rights violations and colonial occupation. The State of Israel was paid reparations by the German state, but, the present political leadership in Israel turned their backs on peace and sought to turn the city of Jerusalem into a militarized centre. The recent mass killings in the occupied territories reinforce the position that there must be long-term peace and a new mode of politics.[48]

The lessons of the genocide in Rwanda and Burundi, war, hunger and bondage in the Sudan and the failure of the African governing classes to increase the respect for human life complicate and enrich the debate on reparations. These struggles against genocide and genocidal violence ensure that the struggle to transcend the ethics and values of the enlightenment and the devaluation of African life is not a racial project. This has been most manifest in the society of Burundi where extremists deploy the same concepts of inferiority and superiority to perpetuate an avalanche of murders and massacres. It is in societies such as Burundi, Rwanda and the Sudan where there is the search for *moral renewal* so that there are fundamental values that ensure dignity and equal protection under the law for all citizens.[49]

What kind of Pan African partnership is possible?

In 1948 C.L.R. James wrote on the barbarism of capitalism in this way: 'The unending murders, the destruction of peoples, the brutal passions, the sadism, the cruelties and the lust, all the manifestations of barbarism of the past thirty years are unparalleled in history. But this barbarism exists because nothing else can oppress the readiness to sacrifice, the democratic instincts and creative power of the masses of the people.'

It is the recognition of the democratic instincts and the creative powers of the people that the purveyors of neo-liberalism seek to harness. This barbarism is disguised as the neo-liberal project of expanding markets and privatization. This disguise takes the form of a democratization exercise that links democracy to elections and a number of parties. One of the tasks of democratizing information is to bring to light the past experiences of destabilization and destruction. The same US government that was at the forefront of military destabilization cannot go forward without moral cleansing of itself in relation to the crimes against Africans. In March 2000, the Pope made an important step in the direction admitting crimes of the past. The Pope asked the world for forgiveness in relation to the past crimes of the church including the inquisition, the forced conversions of peoples in Africa and in America, the support for the crusade and the silence in relation to the Holocaust. Africans all over the world are supporting this moral cleansing with the call for reparations.

This call, especially the appeal for moral reparations, is calling for a thorough re- evaluation of the crimes of capitalism against Africans. The US government is most active in resisting the call for reparations.

The reparation movement in Africa and among Africans overseas has slowly begun to raise the historical genocide of Europeans that has in the past been justified in the name of progress. This call for moral reparations is slowly developing and clarifying the reality that many of the crimes committed by the colonial powers fall under the UN Convention against genocide. The campaign against genocide is necessary in light of the present planning for genetic engineering.

Genocide and biological warfare in the 21st century. Can the Pan-African movement learn the lessons of biological warfare?

This question is very relevant in the context of the present war on terrorism and the debates on weapons of mass destruction. While there is much speculation in certain Western countries (such as the USA and Britain) about attacking countries with weapons of mass destruction (so called Axis of Evil) there is not enough transparency by the same governments in the area of research into biological and chemical weapons. There is great need for Truth and Reconciliation Commissions in the USA and Western Europe.

Through the South African Truth and Reconciliation Commission detailed evidence was presented on nuclear program, the destabilization, the disinformation and psychological warfare and the biological warfare program of the South African Government. Wouter Basson was the head of the special biological and chemical warfare program known as Project Coast. The hearings of the Truth and Reconciliation Commission in South Africa heard evidence (in camera) of the extensive biological warfare program and this author considers it important to reproduce its introduction in full:

The Commission's hearings into South Africa's Chemical and Biological warfare program (the CBW Programme also known as Project Coast) during the 1980's and early 1990's were held in Cape Town in 1998. The hearings focused on the apparently offensive (as opposed to defensive) aspects of the Programme. The image of white-coated scientists, professors, doctors, dentists, veterinarians, laboratories, universities and front companies, propping up apartheid with the support of an extensive international network, was a particularly chilling and cynical one. Here was evidence of science being subverted to cause disease and undermine the health of communities. Cholera, botulism, anthrax, chemical poisoning and the large-scale manufacture of drugs of abuse allegedly for purposes of crowd control were amongst the projects of the Programme. Moreover, chemicals, poisons and lethal micro-organisms were produced for use against individuals and 'applicators' (murder weapons) developed for their administration.[50]

The TRC continued:

The CBW Programme that was developed and supported by scientists, health professionals, research laboratories and front companies, fell under the nominal control of the Surgeon–General of the armed forces. Ostensibly designed and conducted to support a defense capability in response to perceived external threats and international developments, the CBW Programme displayed numerous bizarre aberrations of policy, management and intent. Overall approval and budget control lay with a central management committee that included the

Chief of Staff of the defense force, the Chief of Staff of intelligence, the Surgeon General as project manager and the project leader, Dr. Wouter Basson.[51]

Because the project director was involved in a criminal case, the full details of the biological warfare program to the Truth and Reconciliation Commission was only the tip of the iceberg. The South African courts have since set Basson free. The racial ideas of white superiority induced the whole scientific community in South Africa to participate in this program to develop a *'bacteria that would kill pigmented people – blacks - but not affect whites.'* This Project established a special company where toxic substances would be tested on animals to develop chemical weapons and-most importantly- to develop an immunological fertility drug, which could be used secretly to reduce the birth rate of black people. In this same project, enough cholera was produced to start a major epidemic, potentially lethal weapons such as anthrax was applied to cigarettes and put into drinks-T shirts were laced with cantharidene, a strong irritant, and distributed at an end conscription campaign.[52]

The new armies of Africa, especially those of Zimbabwe, Namibia and South Africa did not seek to develop scientists, engineers, and the kind of skilled cadre that could deal with the new forms of combat of the Twenty-First Century. In fact, in an effort to forestall such commitment, the British Government offered training to most of the new armies when the conditions of liberation required a new military training and thinking. To the knowledge of this author, there is no army in Southern Africa with an Epidemic Intelligence Service. The impact of the HIV pandemic in Africa would have required a total onslaught by all sections of the society to deal with health issues: but the governments are still able to mobilize resources to fight wars but when it comes to health, they seek external assistance.

Whether, the actions of the British and the US in their

orientation and training of African military constitute a conscious attempt to divert attention from biological and chemical warfare, the reality is that the African armies and societies of today are not capable of handling the potential dangers which could occur from outbreak of dangerous viruses. (Leonard Horowitz, *Emerging Viruses: Aids and Ebola: Nature, Accident or Intentional*) There is the need to study the full effects of biological and chemical warfare to develop both civilian and military biohazard experts who concentrate on the present diseases which are occurring in Africa but which are unknown to the traditional doctors.

The co-operation between traditional doctors, scientists, civilian agencies and the military will be crucial in the future of Africa. Integrating military doctors and paramedics into a fight against biological warfare would be one crucial way of restructuring the US military medical mission to Africa. Inside the US, the military has been organized to deal with medical emergencies. Through the Disease Research, Surveillance, Isolation and Containment centers, the US has been studying the ebola virus since this virus is seen as one of the Phantom Warriors presenting a threat to the national security of the USA. It is significant that HIV is presented as one of the Phantom Warriors.

The present proliferation of international agencies focusing on biological warfare has brought out information that in the fifties, African Americans were exposed to potentially fatal stimulant of race specific fungal weapons. Before 1969 when the US government banned the development of offensive biological weapons, there were various lethal bacteria that were being developed in order to identify the character of various viruses that could be effective battlefield weapon. Though the government banned the development of new weapons in 1969, there has not been enough public exposure of what has happened to those viruses that had been developed.

In the history of Western modern medicine, it is known that Africans have been used as guinea pigs. The democratization of information on the viruses that had been developed before 1969 will be a concrete example of partnership with Africa. The kind of cooperation in the future will unearth the extent to which the ideas of eugenics in the USA still exercise a powerful inspiration for the mainstream scientific community. The relationship between eugenics and biological warfare from the period of Adolph Hitler is one of tremendous military significance.

It is now well established that the present genetic engineering tools are by definition, eugenics instruments. Eugenics had been popularized in the USA in the deepening of the pseudo-science of race and racial classification that developed in the wake of Social Darwinism. Positive eugenics has been described as selective "breeding" to improve the characteristics of an organism or species. Negative eugenics involved the systematic elimination of so called undesirable biological traits. Wouter Bassoon's work in South Africa followed the Hitlerian tradition of negative eugenics in seeking to eliminate sections of the African population using biological and chemical agents. African peace researchers will have to have the training to combat the negative eugenics ideas that are influencing the new genetic engineering tools.

Rifkin described this negative eugenics in this way,

Whenever recombination DNA, cell fusion and other related technologies are used to "improve" the genetic blueprints of a microbe, plant, animal or human being, a eugenics consideration is built into the process itself. In laboratories across the globe, molecular biologists are making daily choices about what genes to alter insert and delete from the hereditary code of various species. These are eugenic decisions. Every time a genetic chain of this kind is made, the scientist, corporation, or state is implicitly, if not explicitly making decisions about which are the good genes that should be inserted and preserved and which are the bad genes that should be altered or deleted. This is exactly what eugenics is all abort. Genetic engineering is technology designed to enhance the genetic inheritance of living things by manipulating their genetic code.[53]

Genetic engineering in the present period provides the perfect vehicle for extending the pseudo-science of apartheid. Without democratic control over major projects such as the Human Genome Project, the prospect of discriminatory genotyping of the kind that was being experimented in South Africa could become a reality. As scientists gain more information on the workings of the human genome, they will succeed in identifying an increasing number of genetic traits and predispositions that are unique to specific ethnic and racial groups opening the door to the possibility of genetic discrimination against entire peoples.

In both Africa and in the dispersed African communities, the use of the new technologies to control the reproductive capacities of African women has given rise to critical studies by African feminists on the military consequences of the new technologies in relation to the fertility and reproduction of Africans. The current rave of seeking genetic explanations for human behavior minimizes the history of colonialism, genocide and exploitation. Military applications of genetic engineering are of special significance for this century. Black women are bringing out the tremendous investment in whiteness that is going on at the present investment in what is considered good looks. In the book *Killing the Black Body* the author argued that,

The Human Genome Initiative, an ongoing project to map the complete set of genetic instructions is the largest biology venture in the history of science…... Scientists are attempting to detect genetic markers that indicate a predisposition to complex conditions and behaviors as well as single gene disorders. They anticipate creating genetic tests that will be able to predict a person's susceptibility to haemophilia, mental illness, heart disease etc.[54]

Dorothy Roberts continued,

More disturbing, researchers claim to have discovered not simply the genetic origins of medical conditions, but also the biological explanations for social conditions. Our ability to tinker with the genes children inherit, as well as the belief that gene determines human nature, exaggerates the importance of genes in defining personal identity, and consequently the importance of genetic connections.[55]

The author then went on to outline how African American youth are supposedly predisposed genetically to crime. These are the major battles of the technological development and the debasement of human beings.

African youths liberation and peace

The struggles for peace and the multiple approaches to reconstruction are taking place in a world that is more insecure than at any period since World War II. The global fight against terrorism has instilled values of militarism that reinforce the masculinist ideas of patriarchal societies. The values of patriarchy, violence and plunder are communicated to youths through the instruments of global psychological warfare. Psychological warfare and information warfare attack the minds of the young so that millions of youths are socialized to glorify violence and killings. Throughout the urban and rural areas of Africa, the crisis of reproduction is most manifest in the anti-social values of individualism, greed and the ethics of fighting that is embedded in deformed masculinity. All across the continent, the ethics and values of capitalism and greed have created monsters that keep the majority of their communities hostages. Males are socialized into a violent culture. The young males that are excluded from the pyramidical educational system are dumped on the heap of unemployment and become cannon fodder for military entrepreneurs.

Yet it is from the same ranks of the youth where there are young people emerging to define the tasks of the African Union. In particular, this paper highlighted the agency of African women in the struggles for peace. Precisely because the brunt of the exploitation falls on African women, they have emerged as the force with the most to gain from peace, the African Union and moral reparations.

Throughout Africa, the young and old African women have been producing a new kind of leadership at the grassroots. They have been able to demonstrate that there are new sites for the production of leaders and that these sites can be created in the midst of the most severe crisis. This is the essence of the new peace movement all across Africa —a movement that is slowly taking shape as "the new leaders" bring more wars. The experience of the leadership of Ethiopia and Eritrea in the past five years has clarified the exhaustion of the masculine leadership and the concept of peace that is based on fighting for territorial integrity and sovereignty. It is now clearer that the concept of sovereignty must be based on the sovereignty of the people and not the sovereignty of governments.[56]

The priority accorded to the discussions between the leaders of South Africa, Senegal and Nigeria with the G7 on NEPAD reinforce the conviction of African grassroots organizations that these leaders continue to view economic renewal and peace as an imported commodity. Our intervention sought to critique the realist paradigm and to bring to the forefront the importance of *peace as a process* and the interconnections between peace, justice, healing, reconciliation and economic reconstruction. One deficiency of this discussion has been the inadequate attention paid to the articulation of peace within the struggles against bioterrorism and information warfare. The important conceptual point is that these aspects of insecurity are part of an overall chain of militarism and capital accumulation.

The reformulation of peace and harnessing the creative energies of the people is emerging in a situation where it is becoming clear that peace cannot be an imported commodity based on the landing of troops from international peacekeepers. Most of the peace agreements that have been made in Africa have been platforms for more war and violence. It is this violent history of *war as peace* that is forging the conceptual break with realist principles of politics and the view that might is right.[57]

An alternative vision of peace that brings back the Pan-African principle that "the African is responsible for the well being of his brother and sister and that every African should carry this responsibility" is being enshrined in the transition from the OAU to the African Union and in the activities of the African Descendants Caucus of the World Conference Against Racism (WCAR) process. It is this process that provides one chain in the link between the search for peace in Africa with the global struggles for peace. While the OAU had enshrined principles of "territorial integrity" and 'sovereignty of states' the Constitutive Act of the African Union underlines the dignity and rights of the

African peoples. The Constitutive Act of the Union seeks to move from the idea of 'non interference in the internal affairs of states' to one that spells out the necessity to prevent genocide, crimes against humanity and unconstitutional military interventions. This change that was manifest in the call for non-recognition of governments that came to power by military coups (after 1999) was a significant step in the demilitarization of Africa. African women who have been campaigning for peace have been the strongest and most resilient forces championing new concepts of politics, citizenship and peace.[58]

The implicit ideal that is now on the agenda is that philosophy that defends human life and defends the quality of the lives of the producers. There is now the explicit view that there must be self-reflection in relation to wars and genocidal violence and that one cannot oppose the traditions of colonialism, slavery and apartheid while implementing the very economic basis of colonialism and apartheid. It is now the position of those who are seeking new leadership, that the idea of being recognized as a human being and a human being with dignity is impossible for the African in the present global economy.

This recognition is sharpening the understanding of emancipatory politics and starts from the premise that Africans think, are human beings, and, that the economic and moral values of social collectivism can be the basis for rapid transformation. These ideas are providing the basis for the training of a new leadership cadre and there is the understanding that this training can be carried out in the community, in the mbongi, the village, the school, the church, and the mosque and at sites of cultural renewal. In short, the principles of peace must be built on African concepts of peace or the palavering principle.

Information revolution and peace

The short-term tasks of unity of Africa are tied to the long term tasks of emancipation. Whether it is in Lagos, Dakar, Cairo, London, Los Angeles, Rio, Kingston or Soweto, the youths are at the forefront of resistance. It seems to me that with the rising unemployment, daily racist attacks against the people, the destruction of the educational system and the criminalization of the youth, there is no alternative but to raise the cry of the ancestors who found numerous ways to register opposition to injustice.

The women of Africa and the West are redefining Pan-Africanism. In their daily lives they are exposing the hollowness of trying to catch up and surpass Europe. In every continent it is these same women who have defied the economic laws by developing new skills to survive and to support themselves and their families. Unfortunately, the plans for the future economic regions of Africa are conceived of in the same context of male-centered politics, ignoring the shift of power in the real market place in Africa. Under the banner of privatization and liberalization many people have lost the secure means of reproducing themselves. The phenomenon of street children and child prostitution all across the continent expose the loss of the fundamental values of social solidarity that had been the basis of the African community.

The international financial institutions preach of mythical market forces, ignoring the real commercial expertise displayed by men and women. Foreign monopoly interests continue to dominate, but the future of Africa will develop with the mobilization of the creativity and energy of the people. This principle is based on the reality that if Africans do not control the means of survival and protection, the forces of colonialism will return in the guise of humanitarian workers to rob the continent of the limited independence that was won in the twentieth century.

There can be no democracy, no justice, and no peace, without struggle. The Pan-Africanists of tomorrow will have to defend not only the freedom of those on the continent but Africans in all parts of the world. In this sense, the Pan-Africanism of tomorrow will return to the central dynamic behind the global Pan-African movement, that is no black person is free until all black people are free. It will also have to rise above the European conception of racial classification.

In the words of African-American leader of the 19th century Frederick Douglas,

> the struggle may be a moral one, or it may be a physical one; or it may be both moral and physical, but it must be a struggle. Power concedes nothing without demand. It never did and it never will. Find out just what people will submit to and you have found the exact amount of injustice and wrong that will be imposed upon them, and these will continue until they are resisted with either words or blow or with both. The limits of tyrants are prescribed by the endurance of those whom they oppress.[59]

These words were written in the middle of the fight against slavery in the 19th century. It will be necessary to study the life of Africans such as Frederick Douglas and Harriet Tubman to learn how the people responded to militarism and warfare in the fight for freedom.

The struggle for renewal and emancipatory politics in Africa involves the struggle for democracy and a democratic state that deals with the management of diversity in the society. The basic principle is that in multi-ethnic and multilingual societies of Africa, the ideas of homogenous political rule lead to the politicization of regionalism and ethnicity. The African population is divided along numerous lines.

The concept of Africa for the period of anti-colonialism was based on a view that defied the rich cultural differences between all parts of the continent. It is time to recognize the differences, not to recognize and exacerbate conflict, but to harness the wealth of the different cultures of Africa.

There are divisions (between young and old, women and men, traders, widows, various ethnic groups and nationalities, regions, religions, cultures, races etc). The celebration of diversity must be based on management via democratic institutions and by democratic instruments. The management of diversity would lead to an end to the manipulation of the question of citizenship. This is the major challenge in all of the societies where Africans live, whether Brazil, Venezuela, Colombia or Germany. This will be especially crucial in societies such as Guyana and Trinidad.

This management of diversity includes the reorientation of the educational system so that all of the languages of the society will be celebrated, taught, nurtured and given space to develop. This will also mean the striving for intellectual and ideological diversity. One scholar has linked the issues of intellectual diversity to information freedom and cyberdemocracy. The concept of cyberdemocracy is aimed at challenging the fundamental inequalities in the period of the information and communications revolution. This inequality is manifest in what is usually termed the digital divide. Liberal democratic theories reinforce and reproduce the intellectual conditions for deepening and cementing the digital divide in a context where the information revolution offers new opportunities to educate, mobilize and organize. In this way the democratization of information would advance popular participation and expression beyond the limited experiences of democracy based on voting in elections only.

Multi-party democracy and conception of transitions to democracy sow the seeds of greed, local self-determination and other forms of ethnic divisions. Democracy under this model is conceived of as ethnic majorities. The celebration of diversity and emancipatory politics will allow Africans to benefit from the strength of diversity. The recent advances in genetic engineering and the genome project have refocused our attention of the importance of diversity. It is in this sense that the position of the theories of African women on democracy represents a step forward beyond xenophobia and incitement to hatred that has marked the politics of Africa since colonialism.

Throughout the Pan-African World, women have rendered irrelevant the colonial structures that legally defined them as subservient to men. African women, organized and unorganized, have found numerous ways to make their voices heard. Whether it is the women of the Niger Delta who threatened to occupy Oil platforms or market women demonstrating for protection from corrupt officials, women have been organizing in Africa. In particular, since 1988, the African Women's Development and Communication Network (FEMNET) developed an organization for Women in the NGO movement to share information, experiences, ideas and strategies through communications, networking, training and advocacy. FEMNET and other networks have been at the forefront of the campaigns for African governments to ratify the protocols on the rights of women in Africa.   Through the active struggles of women, some states are changing the most oppressive laws relating to the subordination of women, but even when these states change the law; the practices of domination are justified under the name of tradition. Yet, in day-to-day life it is women, especially from the working classes (poor peasants, traders, poor farmers, students, healers and spiritual intercessors) who keep the society together.

Through their daily work, songs, dance, music and other forms of expression the women seek to give voice to the quest for a new mode of politics by creating new sites of politics in the community and in the family. The politicians always seek to co-opt the militancy of the women and one can see this in the efforts of the present governments to co-opt sections of the women and to direct their voices into legitimacy for ruling elements.[60] The struggle for emancipatory politics sharpens the question of the place of women in the struggle for peace and brings squarely the issue of social emancipation away from the ideas of women in development and other formulations that are intended to call on women and to support their domination and self-exploitation. All areas of life, work, leisure, health and biological reproduction have been negatively affected by the patriarchal worldview and now this patriarchy is imprinted in economics and politics.

Globalization and the new voices among Africans.

One of the positive aspects of globalization and the communications revolution has been the struggle by African youth to seek new forms of expression, to oppose the crudeness and barbarity of the system. In the midst of the attempts to dehumanize, the African cultural artists from all sections of the Pan-African world, they create the cultural products: whether reggae, hip hop, soca, Kwasa Kwasa to give voice to the youth. In the Caribbean cultural leaders such as David Rudder have been explicit in his call for the solidarity with the peoples of Cuba. Calls for solidarity with Cuba and Haiti are expressed in many ways. In North America there is a very strong vehicle for Pan-African struggle in the Hip-hop culture.

Exposing the hypocrisy of the system, these youths expose the contradictions of the system and the alienating conditions of urbanization. They are able to spread the ideas of resistance around the world and creatively use the advances in technology to give meaning to their creativity. We can see culture as one of the principal battlegrounds of resistance.

The voices of those calling for emancipatory politics are amplified by the hip-hop nation. The call for emancipation is muted because the hip-hop nation emerges from the visceral nature of the oppression of the youth. It is not by accident that the hip-hop phenomenon emerged out of Bronx (New York) and followed the trail of capital as the voice of resistance. Hip-hop speaks to the youth in the USA, Japan, France, Germany, and Brazil. African hip-hop and cultural expressions are major forces in Pan-African politics.

Today, hip-hop is considered one of the must successful musical innovations and global cultural forces since the emergence of rock 'n' roll in the 1950's. Hip-hop music expresses the attitudes of a generation of youth that lived a hostile existence in American urban centers. Across the globe, youth are embracing hip-hop culture and using it to express their social realities. Hip-hop culture belongs in the discourse of globalization because it is a process that has transformed the oratory and music of urban Black and Latino youth in America into a transnational, hybrid form of music and cultural expression among youth outside the USA. In dress, speech, dance, and music this resistance speaks to humanity. There is both the positive and negative element to this music. There is the way in which the music industry tries to commodify this culture. The American music entertainment industry and advances in digital music storage and distribution technology, such as INTERNET and MP3 technology determine the nature of hip-hop as a cultural commodity.

But despite this commodification the voice of resistance emerges. Witness the rise of Lauryn Hill to the top of the entertainment field singing 'one love.' The song represented one arena of expression. Other arenas were seized in sports. Whether in the field of tennis, golf, basketball, track and field and soccer, young Africans are making their mark in the international arena. In the Caribbean, the ebb and flow of the participation in international cricket tournaments is of particular relevance.

During the colonial era, Barbadian and other Caribbean peoples seized the arena of cricket as a major arena of struggle. C.L.R. James in his book, *Beyond the Boundary* has already brought to the attention of the peoples of the Caribbean the linkage of cricket to black dignity. Numerous intellectuals since that time have raised the issues of the cultural and political lessons of the game of cricket. There have also been cricketers such as Alfie Roberts of St.Vincent and Vivian Richards of Antigua who consciously supported the Pan-African liberation struggle. Rodney Worrell brought out the ways in which issue of playing cricket in South Africa during the era of apartheid was a central issue for the Southern Africa Liberation Committee in Barbados. These lessons of the link between sports, cultural autonomy and self-expression will be important aspects of the Pan-African liberation struggle in the present century. In this century the youths will rise above the simple definitions of race.

This is already evident from the new Pan-African voices. Bob Marley had an English father and an African mother. He clung to his African roots while supporting human liberation. Bob Marley rose above the sterile definition of who is an African. These are the new Pan-African voices. Bob Marley inspired us to move from resistance to transformation. The progressive rap artists have taken up this message in the hip-hop underground.

The seeds of this transformation are being planted and we need the conditions for its growth. From the Congo to Nigeria and from Morocco to the Sudan right down through the continent, the cultural outpourings assert the humanity of the Africans. In songs, music, drumming, art, dance and in all cultural representations there are new voices being heard across the African continent.

Pan-African liberation and emancipation require that we lift new voices and at the same time view the knowledge of our people as basic for future transformation. The recognition of this indigenous knowledge is one thing, but creating a bottom up approach for the humanization of the planet is quite another. This requires an embrace of the *Healing Wisdom of Africa.*

There are two pillars of the culture, the culture of resistance and emancipation and the culture of militarism and destruction. The Healing Wisdom supports the culture of peace and transformation. Intergenerational peace requires the Pan-Africanists to bring out the positive aspects of the popular culture while exposing the negative.

African women who are daughters of the goddess are breaking the ideas of masculine power and are slowly training a new cadre of leaders whose task is to *let life live.* This is the new philosophy of human dignity that has great potential for not only the emancipation of the African, but for the return of the dignity of all human beings. The ethic of social collectivism and the morality of a decent life for all are being spread by those voices that are singing the songs of emancipation from mental slavery.

Bob Marley is calling for emancipation from mental slavery as the basis of cooperation.

Horace Campbell
Professor of African American Studies and Political Science
Syracuse University, May 25, 2002.

Notes

[1] See details of the *Constitutive Act of the African Union*.

[2] For an in-depth analysis of the possible impact of the war on terrorism on Africans in all parts of the world, see interview in Blackelectorate.com, October 25, 2001.

[3] Angela Davis, "Race and Criminalization: Black Americans and the Punishment Industry," edited by Wahneema Lubiano, *The House That Race Built: Black Americans, U.S. Terrain* (New York: Pantheon Books, 1997).

[4] For details of the BRC campaign see http://www.blackradicalcongress.org/education.html.

[5] Jonas Savimbi was the leader of a movement called UNITA in Angola. This movement was started in 1964. At that time there were three liberation movements, MPLA, FLNA and UNITA. However, in after the fall of the fascist government in Portugal in 1974 Jonas Savimbi and UNITA became an open ally of the apartheid regime of South Africa. After independence in 1975 this leader waged war in the countryside unleashing untold destruction. Even those who celebrated his fight on behalf of the USA and South Africa have been forced to write about the atrocities that he carried out in Angola. For an account see Horace Campbell, *Militarism, Warfare and the Search for Peace in Angola* (Pretoria: Africa Institute, 2001).

[6] Kwame Nkrumah, *Africa Must Unite* (New York: International Publishers 1972).

[7] Michael E. Veal, *Fela: The Life and Times of an African Musical Icon* (Philadelphia: Temple University Press, 2000).

[8] The Act of Union embraces 53 countries in Africa. Morocco has not joined the African Union and has applied for membership in the European Union.

[9] The NEPAD Initiative that was launched at the 2001 OAU summit was a merger between the Millennium Partnership for the African Recovery Program (MAP) and the Omega Plan.

[10] See the African Development Bank Group- African Civil Society Regional Stakeholders Consultation on New Partnership For Africa's Development, Abijan, Cote D'Ivorie (4-5 April, 2002). See also the Bamako Declaration of African Social Forum (January 5-9, 2002).

[11] Walter Rodney, "Towards the Sixth Pan African Congress,"

in Horace Campbell, ed, *Pan-Africanism: The struggle against imperialism and neo-colonialism: documents of the Sixth Pan African Congress*, (Toronto: Afro-Carib Publications, 1975).

[12] Ifi Amadiume, *Daughters of the Goddess: Daughters of Imperialism*(London: Zed Books, 2000) and Patricia McFadden, "Impunity, Masculinity and Heterosexism in the Discourse of male Endangerment: An African Feminist Perspective(Working Paper Series, Center For Gender and Development Studies, University of the West Indies, No.7, March 2002).

[13] These points emerged from a summary session of a conference held at the University of the West Indies at St. Augustine to celebrate the life of Henry Sylvestre Williams and the one hundredth anniversary of the First Pan African Congress in 1900.

[14] For an elaboration of the elements of the patriarchal model of liberation see Horace Campbell, *Reclaiming Zimbabwe: The Exhaustion of the Patriarchal Model of Liberation* (Trenton: Africa World Press 2003).

[15] Thandika Mkandawire, *Our Continent, Our Future: African Perspectives on Structural Adjustment* (Trenton: Africa World Press, 2000).

[16] Walter Rodney, *How Europe Underdeveloped Africa* (Dar Es Salaam: Tanzania Publishing House, 1972) and Bruce Vandervort, *Wars of Imperial Conquest in Africa*, 1830-1914(Bloomington: Indiana University Press, 1998).

[17] Quoted in Cecilia Green, *Reclaiming Women's Lives, Against the Current* (September /October 1992).

[18] Susantha Goonatilake, *Toward a global science*: *Mining Civilizational Knowledge* (Bloomington: Indiana University Press, 1998).

[19] Sandra G. Harding, *The 'Racial' Economy of Science: Towards a Democratic Future* (Bloomington: Indiana University Press, 1998).

[20] Fritjof Capra, *The Turning Point: Science, Society and the Rising Culture* (New York: Simon and Schuster, 1982).

[21] Samir Amin, *Eurocentrism* (New York: Monthly Review Press, 1989). In this book Samir Amin interrogated the basic premises of the intellectual project of the enlightenment but he did not go deeper in to the limitations of Newtonian physics.

[22] William H. Watkins, "Pan-Africanism and the Politics of Education, Towards a New Understanding," in *Imaging Home: Class, Culture and Nationalism in the African Diaspora* (London: Verso Books,

1994. See also Ngugi Wa Thiongo, *Decolonizing the Mind*, (Portsmouth: Heinemann, 1986) and Carter G Woodson, *The MisEducation of the Negro* (, Trenton: Africa World Press, 1990).

[23] This class has been discussed at length in Frantz Fanon, *Black Skin, White Masks* (New York: Grove Press, 1967).

[24] Philip Gourevitch, *We Wish to Inform You that Tomorrow We will be killed along with our families: Stories from Rwanda* (New York: Farrar, Straus and Giraux, 1998) and Mahmood Mamdani, *When Victims Become Killer* (Princeton University Press, 2001).

[25] Cathy Cohen, *Boundaries of Blackness: AIDS and the Breakdown of Black Politics* (Chicago: University of Chicago Press, 1999).

[26] The concept of the feedback loop is a characteristic of the recursion principle of fractals. Ron Eglash, *African Fractals: Modern Computing and Indigenous Design* (New Brunswick: Rutgers University Press, 1999).

[27] Sidney J. Lemelle and Ifi Ni Owoo, *Pan Africanism for Beginners* (New York: Readers and Writers, 1992). For an early history of Pan Africanism, see Vincent B Thompson, *Africa and Unity: The Evolution of Pan Africanism* (London: Longmans, 1969). See also Bernard Magubane, *The Ties That Bind: African American Consciousness of Africa* (Trenton: Africa World Press, 1978).

[28] P.O.Esedebe, *Pan Africanism: The Idea and the Movement*(Washington: Howard University Press, 1982) and Immanuel Geiss, *The Pan-African movement; a history of Pan-Africanism in America, Europe, and Africa*, Africana Publishing House, New York, 1974).

[29] Walter Rodney, "The Imperialist Partitioning of Africa," *Monthly Review* (April 1970). See also Walter Rodney, *How Europe Underdeveloped Africa* (Dar Es Salaam: Tanzania Publishing House, 1972).

[30] C.L.R James, *A History of Pan African Revolts* (Chicago: Charles H Kerr, 1995).

[31] Micere Mugo, "Re-envisioning Pan Africanism: What is the Role of Gender, Youth and the Masses?" in *Pan* Africanism and Integration in Africa, edited by Ibbo Mandaza and Dan Nabudere(Harare: Sapes Books, 2002). See also Lisa Aubrey, "Towards a pan-African view of Women and (Co) Development Considering Race in the Era of Development NGOs , " *CODESRIA Bulletin*, No 1, 1997.

[32] *Walter Rodney Speaks: the making of an African Intellectual*

(Africa World Press: Trenton, 1990).

[33] The proposition that there was a miracle in the negotiations to end apartheid has been propagated by Allister H Sparks, *Tomorrow is Another Country: The Inside Story of South Africa's Road to Change* (New York: Hill and Wang, 1995). For two alternative interpretations of the anti apartheid struggle see Horace Campbell, "Challenging The Apartheid System From Below, " in Anyang' Nyong'o, P. (ed.), *Popular Struggles for Democracy in Africa*(Zed Books: London, 1988) and Barbara Hutmacher MacLean, *Strike a woman, Strike a rock: Fighting for Freedom in South Africa*(Trenton: Africa World Press, 2004).

[34] Umoren, Uduakobong E., "The symbolism of the Nigerian women's war of 1929: an anthropological study of an anti-colonial struggle," *African Study Monographs* 16 (1995) 2, 61-72. See also, Sembene Ousmane, *Gods Bits of Wood* (Portsmouth: Heinemann, 1978).

[35] Walter Rodney, "Towards the 6th Pan-African Congress: Aspects of the International Class Struggle in Africa, America and the Caribbean" in Horace Campbell (ed) *Pan-Africanism: Documents of the Sixth Pan*-African Congress (Toronto: Afro-Carib Publications, 1975).

[36] See Declaration of the *First Pan-African Women's Conference on A Culture for Peace and Non-Violence,* Zanzibar 17-20 May 1999. Also see Fatima Babiker, "Pan Africanism and The Liberation of African Women" in Tajudeen Abdul Raheem, *Pan Africanism: Politics, Economy and Social Change in the Twenty-first Century,* (New York: New York University 1996).

[37] Quoted in *Let Nobody Turn us Around: Voices of Resistance, Reform and Renewal,* edited by Manning Marable and Leith Mullings (New York Rowman and Littlefield Publishers, 2000).

[38] Phillipe Wamba, *Kinship: a family's journey in Africa and America* (New York: Dutton, 1999).

[39] Horace Campbell "Pan-Africanism in the Twenty-First Century" in Tajudeen Abdul- Raheem, *Pan-Africanism: Politics, Economy and Social Change in the Twenty-First Century* (New York: New York University Press, 1996).

[40] Patricia MC Fadden, "Impunity, Masculinity and Heterosexism in the Discourse on Male Endangerment: An African Feminist Perspective, (*Working Paper*, No. 7. Centre For Gender and

Development Studies, University of the West Indies, Cave Hill, March 2002).

[41] Eusi Kwayana Unpublished Lecture 1993.

[42] Ibid.

[43] Jeremy Rifkin, *The Biotech Century: Harnessing the Gene and Remaking the World* (New York: Putman Books, 1999).

[44] Vandana Shiva, *Biopiracy: The Plunder of Nature and Knowledge (*Boston: South End Press, 1997).

[45] Patricia McFadden, "Impunity, Masculinity and Heterosexism in the Discourse on Male Endangerment: An African Feminist Perspective," 31

[46] Adam Hochschild, *King Leopold's Ghost: a story of greed, terror, and heroism in colonial Africa*, (Boston: Houghton Miflin, 1998).

[47] Ludo De Witte, *The Assassination of Patrice Lumumba* (New York: Verso Books, 2001).

[48] Michel Chossudovsky, *The Globalization of Poverty*: *impacts of IMF and World Bank reforms*, (London: Zed books, 1997).

[49] For an elaboration of he search for these values in the context of the Burundi Peace Process see, *Arusha Peace and Reconciliation Agreement for Burundi*, Arusha, August 2000.

[50]Truth and Reconciliation Commission of South Africa, Vol 2 Chapter 6, South Africa's Chemical and Biological Warfare Programme, Final Report, presented to President Nelson Mandela, October 1998

[51] Ibid.

[52] Ibid.

[53] Jeremy Rifkin. Ibid.

[54] Dorothy Roberts, *Killing the Black Body: Race, Reproduction and the Meaning of Liberty* (New York: Vintage Books, 1999).

[55] Ibid.

[56] Wamba dia Wamba, "Zaire: From the National Conference to the Federal Republic of the Congo? *Development Dialogue*, No. 2 (1995).

[57] Horace Campbell, "The Peace Narrative and Education For Peace in Africa," in *The Political Economy of Peace in Africa*, edited by Adele Jinadu, (Harare: AAPS, 2000). See also, Michael Maren, *The Road to Hell*, (New York: The Free Press, 1998).

[58] Zanzibar Declaration of The Pan African Women working for a Culture of Peace (May 1999).

[59] The Frederick Douglas papers (New Haven: Yale University Press, 1979)157.

[60] The mobilization of women to serve the interests of governments is discussed at length by Ifi Amadiume, Daughters of the Goddess: Daughters of Imperialism, Zed Books, London, 200. See also Amina Mama, "Feminism or Femocracy? State Feminism and Democratization in Nigeria," in *Africa Development*. CODESRIA, Vol.XX, No.1, 1995.

Leroy Harewood:
Pan-African Humanist

By Rodney Worrell

Introduction

In 2002, a number of Pan-African organizations in Barbados including: the Clement Payne Movement, African Reparations, Pan-African Movement of Barbados, Israel Lovell Foundation and the Commission For Pan-African Affairs came together (Emancipation Committee) to put on a number of activities to celebrate the Season of Emancipation. The Emancipation Committee decided to stage the Leroy Harewood Memorial Lecture, in recognition of the outstanding contribution Leroy Harewood made to Pan-Africanism and socialism in Barbados. I was asked to deliver this historic lecture (at the Israel Lovell Foundation on the 23rd of July 2002). The reader should hear the voice of a Barbadian Pan-Africanist; the frequent quotations should be able to bring Leroy Harewood voice to the fore.

Introductory greetings

Greetings Comrades! I give kudos to the organizers—David Denny and the Emancipation Committee of Barbados for having the vision and foresight to convene this inaugural Leroy Harewood Memorial Lecture. It is imperative that as Pan-Africanists we seek to canonize and pay homage to our heroes; our valiant soldiers - who have made invaluable contributions in the protracted struggle for the dignity and human rights of the oppressed at home and worldwide. Moreover, it is our duty to educate fellow comrades and the wider public in Barbados, the Caribbean and elsewhere, about the contributions of our heroes. It is a pleasure, an honor and a challenge to give this address on "Leroy Harewood, Pan-African Humanist." Some time in the early nineties, I was fascinated with the excerpts of an address given by Leroy Harewood - I think it was the Rudolph Goodridge Memorial Lecture - the tone of his address reminded me of the revolutionary fervor in the writings of Frantz Fanon, George Jackson, H. Rap Brown and the Black Panthers.

At the very outset, I must warn you that this lecture is not historical or biographical, but one that examines Harewood's social and political thoughts. Leroy Harewood was born on April 2, 1932, and he made the transition to the ancestors on February 21, 1994. It is my contention that Leroy Harewood is the greatest Barbadian Pan-Africanist of the late twentieth century. Indeed he belongs to the transformative school of Pan-Africanism, and stood firmly in the tradition of C.L.R. James, George Padmore, Kwame Toure, W.E.B. Du Bois, Kwame Nkrumah, Walter Rodney, Manning Marable, Nanny Grig, Angela Davis, Assata Shankur, Amy Jacques Garvey, Elma Francois and Horace Campbell. Leroy Harewood was an organic intellectual, not in the elite theory of intellectuals or the occupational categories; but as someone who was concerned with the 'criticism, transmission and evaluation, of the principles by which society is supposed to be governed.' He believed that it was his 'bounden duty to betray the calling fate had determined' and 'put his knowledge and skills' at the disposal of the black working class, in defense of this section of the population. During Harewood's first sojourn in Britain, he edited a radical newspaper called the *Monthly Torch*. On his return to Barbados he joined the Peoples Progressive Movement (PPM) a Marxist political party and became the editor of the *Black Star* newspaper, where he sought to give voice to the voiceless and highlighted the issues that affected the black masses. In this process Harewood became an uncompromising fighter and champion of the black underclass locally and internationally. This was also evident when he edited the *New Vision* the short lived organ of the Pan-African Movement of Barbados; in his articles for the *Pulse* newspaper; and as a member of the Clement Payne Movement where he continued to address several issues affecting the black working class.

Who are Africans?

Leroy Harewood, in the intellectual Pan-Africanists tradition of Martin Delaney, Edward Blyden, W.E.B. Du Bois, Marcus Garvey and Walter Rodney recognized the value of utilizing African historical knowledge as a weapon in the protracted struggle against white supremacy. Many years ago Marcus Garvey warned:

> White Historians and writers have tried to rob the black man of his proud past in history and when anything new is discovered to support the race's claim and to attest of greatness in other ages, and then it is skillfully rearranged and credited to some other unknown race or people.[1]

In taking up the polemical challenge of seeking to free the minds of persons of African ancestry from the centuries of falsifications, lies and distortions; Harewood raised a number of questions that are still relevant and are constantly being debated in Barbados and the wider African

Diaspora: i) Who are black people? ii) Where did we come from? and iii) Where are we going?

In answering the above questions, Harewood stated, 'that we are descendants of Africans,' who were taken from Africa by 'European marauders to work as slaves on the sugar plantations of the Americas.' Moreover, he emphatically stated that the African people had a great culture and were a very 'proud people who constructed arguably the world's greatest civilization.'[2] However, today black people are second-class citizens in the West Indies, who still suffer racial persecution, and whose labor is still enriching a handful of white traitors—are the descendants of the people who built the first communist societies in the world (primitive communalism). What impressed Harewood about African communalism was the egalitarianism and humanism of African traditional society. In African traditional societies no private property existed—the people owned the land, and the crops were divided among the people. Indeed it was even asserted that 'certain African communities ate out of a common pot.' Harewood asked what happened to change all of this. How a people that had constructed this wonderful civilization, had sunk so low and are now struggling against poverty, ignorance and backwardness.

> How come so many millions of descendants of a once proud people could be so degraded as to want to change even the color of their skin and the texture of their hair? How indeed, did the African come to be reduced to an almost sub-human level not only in the West Indies but also in his own country Africa?[3]

Harewood recognized that globally people of African descent are made to feel inferior and relegated to a second class citizen. This is done by the constant bombardment of Euro-culture, European institutions and European achievements throughout the popular and not so popular media. Black people have been forced by either physical brutality or psychological brutality to conform to European culture. Indeed, the European has an 'inflated and distorted view of his own importance.' 'Everything white is viewed as good and everything black is viewed as bad.' Europe and North America are made to look like the cradles of human civilization, while Africa and Asia are considered the land of the backward races. What distressed Harewood was 'that millions of black people have accepted this lie.' Harewood using the Du Boisan thesis demonstrated that the level of development in Sub-Saharan Africa during the fourteenth century was comparable to that of Europe around the same period. He argued that the Negroid influence was the main influence in Egypt's development from 2100 to 1600 B.C.; and in East, South, and West Africa human culture from 1600 B.C. to A.D 1500, these areas contained monuments of a vigorous past and a growing civilization.[4] John Henrik Clarke asserted that 'the evidence of the Africanness of Nile Valley civilization, the evidence of Egypt being solely and purely African is so clear. The argument is an offense to my intelligence and yours.'[5] And Diop stated that 'according to the unanimous testimony of the Ancients, first the Ethiopians and then the Egyptians created and raised to an extra-ordinary stage of development all the elements of civilization, while other peoples especially the Eurasians, were still deep in Barbarism.'[6] Harewood wondered what changed all this. What killed the Sudanese Empires and brought anarchy and destruction into the Nile valley? What decimated the thick populations of East and Central Africa and crushed the culture of West Africa beneath the ruthless heel of rising European culture? He opines that what retarded Africa's development was the slave trade - racist chattel slavery was the worst form of slavery that ever afflicted mankind.

This trade in human blood and misery was started in 1441 when one Antonio Gonsalivez a Portuguese sea captain kidnapped 12 Africans from the West Coast of Africa and took them to Lisbon and presented them to Prince Henry as slaves. The Prince immediately wrote to the Pope telling him about plans to start the slave trade. The Pope replied ... granting to all of those who shall take part in the said war, complete forgiveness for sins.

Receiving the Pope's blessing the Portuguese now set out on a full time slave raiding expedition all along the coast of Africa. Spain later entered the trade along with Portugal ... they held the monopoly of this bloody trade until about the year 1544 when the French decided to challenge them.

The British were not to close their eyes to the fat profits from the trade; they also joined and very soon became the biggest and most ruthless of the slave traders.

With the crying need for labor also on the islands the slavers became more brutal and inhumane when dealing with our forefathers.

Cruel, bloody and satanic they became slave hunters. This was money; black men, women and children were considered just like cattle and in many cases worse...

It is estimated that for every African that arrived at the coast, five died on the way. For the white men the life of the African was worthless.

All of this helped to wreck the African civilization and put blight on advancement. But this was only the beginning. Worse was in store for the black slaves on the plantation.[7]

While the horrendous atrocities of the middle passage are known by all students of slavery - black men and women being beaten to death; men, women and children that were thrown overboard to feed the sharks; the stench, squalor, misery, brutality and death that were part and parcel of these slave ships. Harewood felt that these atrocities were mild in comparison to the crimes committed against the Africans when they landed in the West Indies. To support this position, he mentioned that the 'African was stripped of his culture, degraded and dehumanized,' this was done to make the African accept the 'intolerable burden of slavery.' The chattlelization of the African made him a 'pitiable human object knowing no country, owning no loyalty to any man but the brutal slave master.' The physical and psychological brutality wreaked havoc with the minds of the exiled Africans. Harewood attributes this brutal treatment for creating the fear, docility, childishness and lack of self-confidence in the mind of the African. He wrote:

It was asserted in Parliament in 1780 in Bridgetown, General Tottenham saw a Negro youth entirely naked who wore round his neck an iron collar with five long projecting spikes. His belly and his thighs were almost cut to pieces, with running ulcers all over and a finger might have been laid in every one of his wounds.

He could not sit down because his hinder parts were mortified and it was impossible for him to lie down on account of the prongs on his collar. He had nearly been whipped to death and then abandoned.

One can imagine the fear this boy may have evoked in the Africans who saw him. But if they were not sufficiently weakened with fear, the white man used another form of brutality to weaken and demoralized the Africans. It was starvation.[8]

Slavery for the African meant something that was much more degrading than being lashed, or raped, or working from morning to night. According to Harewood:

> There was something far more sinister, far more deadly at work on the slave plantations in the West Indies and the Americas. There for the first time in the history of the human race a group of people was trying to reduce another group to brutes fit only for work and to weep.
>
> True the African people were not the first and only people to have been enslaved, but what was new was that white men had enslaved black men.
>
> The slave was always legally at the bottom of the scale. He had the least claims upon consideration and the lowest prerogatives among men. But the slave responsibility was largely legal rather than moral.
>
> The deep significance of African slavery was not that the blacks should be slaves for a period, but rather that they should be slaves forever. The chains may be taken away from the ankles but they had to be placed on their minds.
>
> It was no misfortune that African slaves were constantly degraded and humiliated on the slave plantations. The so-called seasoning process was aimed at making the African permanently inferior to the European. The slave laws maintained that all white people were by their color alone superior to the blacks…[9]

Like Edward Blyden, Eric Williams and Walter Rodney, Harewood forcefully argued that the slave trade and slavery made Britain develop from 'stone age backwardness to be the greatest industrial giant in the world.' He posited:

For over three hundred years, millions of black men groaned under the yoke of racist slavery. In those three hundred years Britain emerged from almost stone-age backwardness to be the greatest industrial giant in the world.

Black slavery made her rich and famous. The groans of the sugar plantations were the long hymns of praise to her; the stench, the misery and the degradation and the wholesale slaughtering of a people both physically and psychologically were like great store houses of wealth.[10]

He agreed with Williams and Marxist historical school that slavery was largely abolished for economic reasons. And like CLR James and Richard Hart, he felt that the frequency of the slave revolts and resistance was very instrumental in forcing the slave owners to abolish slavery. Harewood quoted Du Bois to give some explanation to the abolition of slavery:

Apologists for slavery like to allude to the fact that a number of Europeans opposed slavery and fought to have it abolished. Eric Williams in his "Capitalism and Slavery" has been seriously misunderstood and grossly exaggerated…

Slavery was abolished mainly for economic reasons. The growing frequency of the slave revolts … which had reached intensity after the victorious Haitian Revolution of 1803…

The mortality rate of slaves was increasing at such a rate that the slave masters were finding it difficult to replenish what they called the human livestock.

It is obvious that a system that was established for the maintenance of super profits would not tolerate anything that was to reduce or threaten its sway. The blacks could not be allowed to disappear as the North American Indian or the Caribs of the Caribbean; they were wanted for cheap labor.

...These human masters who had grown fat on the labor of the black slaves could not see how the plantation could function without them. If slavery was abolished, they asked who will compensate us for our slaves – the men, women and children who we had bought and kept like cattle.

The blindness of the slave masters, their mental laziness, their arrogance and their dependence on black men to work for them posed an enormous problem for the abolitionist. They were accused of not knowing the facts about slavery and of exaggeration and distortion.

But Britain and the other slave powers knew slavery had run its course and had to be replaced by a less crude form of enslavement.

...Eventually Negro slavery and the slave trade were abandoned in favor of colonial imperialism, and England which in the Eighteen Century established modern slavery in the Americas on a vast scale appeared as the official emancipator of slaves and the founder of a method of control of human labor and material which proved more profitable than slavery.

Officially, slavery was legally abolished but the damage to the black man's psyche was done. It is this damage that we must seek to repair. Unless we succeed in restoring his health, the black man will remain a pariah and menial in the western world.[11]

Hunger/underdevelopment

Leroy Harewood like all progressives in the quest for social justice wondered why there was Underdevelopment.
Why there was this great divide between the rich and poor?
Why must people die of hunger in a world where milk is
poured down disused mines? Where meat is thrown away
and wheat deliberately destroyed by fire?   He wondered
if there is some evil god that ordains poverty, hunger and
misery for millions and riches for the few. Harewood stated
that global inequality was a by-product of Western capitalism.[12] European capitalists under colonialism and imperialism have ruthlessly exploited the countries of Asia, Africa,
Latin America and the Caribbean. These countries are extremely rich in terms of natural resources, but, their peoples are relatively poor when compared with the peoples
of Western Europe and North America. He recognized that
although most of the countries of the South, are said to be
independent, they are little better than 'colonies who provide raw materials for the industrialized countries of North
America and Europe.'[13]

Walter Rodney as part of the intellectual milieu stated:

> Capitalism has proved incapable of transcending
> fundamental weaknesses such as under utilization
> of productive capacity, the persistence of a perma-
> nent sector of unemployed, and periodic crises re-
> lated to the concept of 'market'- which is concerned
> with people's ability to pay rather than their need
> for commodities. Capitalism has created its own ir-
> rationalities such as vicious white racism, the tre-
> mendous waste associated with advertising, and
> the irrationality of incredible poverty in the midst of
> wealth and wastage even inside the biggest capitalist
> economies, such as the United States of America.[14]

Moreover, Rodney mentions:

In a way, underdevelopment is a paradox. Many
parts of the world that are naturally rich are actu-
ally poor and parts that are not so well off in wealth
of soil or sub-soil are enjoying the highest standard
of living. When capitalists from the developed parts
of the world try to explain this paradox, they often
make it sound that there is something "God given"
about the situation…The interpretation that underdevelopment is somehow ordained by God is em-
phasized because of the racist trend in European
scholarship. It is in line with the racist prejudice to
say openly or to imply that their countries are more
developed because their people are innately superior, and that the responsibility of the backwardness
of Africa lies in the generic backwardness of the race
of black Africans. An even bigger problem is that
the people of Africa and other parts of the colonized
world have gone through a cultural and psychological crisis and have accepted at least partially, the European version of things. That means that the African
himself has doubts about his capacity to transform
and develop his natural environment. With such
doubts he even challenges his brothers who say that
Africa can and will develop through the efforts of its
own people.[15]

Harewood felt that the following devices were used to
see the continuity of hunger and underdevelopment in the
neo-colonies:

1) Puppet governments are propped up by arms from
North America and Europe and installed in most countries
in Africa, Asia, Latin America and the Caribbean.

2) Big banks, insurance companies and foreign firms move into most of the countries to mop up finance and cheap labor.

3) No real development is allowed except the building of tourist resorts, a few window- dressing projects like a little housing area, a new post office, a new highway or a new school.

4) There is no agricultural development.

5) Money to line the pockets of venal and corrupt politicians and trade union leaders- borrowed from foreign banks at exorbitant rates of interests.

6) A high level of unemployment is maintained to provide cheap, docile labor for subsidiaries of big North American firms.

7) A one-crop economy forms the hub of most of the hungry countries economies. And this one crop whether it is sugar, coffee or bananas is controlled by a handful of capitalists, sometimes foreign, sometimes local and foreign. The main point; however is that none of them is interested in the development of the country.

8) Many of the countries insist on trading mainly with Britain, the United States and Canada. Any trade with Eastern Europe is frowned upon; more often it is deliberately stopped.

9) The primary products of the underdeveloped countries are bought by the developed countries for next to nothing. Yet they sell those countries their manufactured goods at very high prices.

10) Ways and means are found to crush all local initiative and to keep the people dependent on foreigners for everything from the making of a pin to the naming of a hospital.[16]

Harewood, within the context of the cold war contestation between capitalism and socialism/communism stated that communism was not responsible for the poverty and economic problems in the Caribbean and Latin America. Furthermore, it was not communism that pays fat salaries to corrupt government officials in Africa, Asia, Latin America and the Caribbean, while children die of hunger in these countries. While it was imperative for these countries to break out of this economic backwardness, Harewood recognized that this task could not be accomplished by words such as 'democracy and dogmoney'—in the form of aid from the Economic North. The solution to escape (out of) this predicament was for the Economic North to pay fair prices for the goods coming from the Economic South, and 'for ruthless progressive governments to liquidate the roots of imperialism.' It was quite clear that poverty and hunger cannot be conquered by following the same old worn path left by the imperialists. What was needed was a vigorous self-reliant, self-survival initiative, where the Third World countries would pool their human and material resources, so as to become less dependent on the imperialists. He strongly resented depending on the Economic North for any real economic assistance, which he likened 'to the lamb depending on the wolf for grass.' Harewood was quite optimistic that the Third World could conquer hunger but the first task of this project was to conquer neo-colonialism and imperialism. How this is done, Harewood posited, will depend on how firm the resistance will be; he wondered whether it would be accomplished by bullets and blood?[17]

The famines and widespread starvation that ravished the Horn of Africa during the late nineteen eighties and early nineties, was a cause of great concern to Harewood. He believed that Africa with its 'extensive land mass and vast natural resources should have a food security system in place to prevent this scale of starvation from taking place.' According to Harewood, Africa, the richest continent in the world has become 'a ragged giant begging for handouts from the Western World.' This level of dependence on the west for aid would certainly erode what little sovereignty was left. Africa's mal-development took place because 'modern Africa has forgotten everything about the past.' What was ironic was the fact that political independence has aggravated rather than provided solutions to Africa's economic woes. The majority of the African countries were now converted into reservoirs of cheap labor, providing one or two export crops, to supply the European, North American or Japanese market.[18]

African leaders, like the state managers in the Caribbean, 'were hell bent on obtaining foreign exchange, therefore the land, labor and even the dignity of the people seemed to be sacrificed to get foreign exchange.' Food production for the people was not seen as important as the production of cocoa, or groundnuts or other primary products for the export market. In addition, the African peasants the primary producers of food were neglected. They received very little assistance with tractors, fertilizers, irrigation facilities and land management. This development led to frustration among the peasants who became attracted to the bright lights of the cities, fast food and brand name clothes made in the United States, leading them to give up farming for life in the slums. The rapid drift from the countryside has been one of the contributing factors of starvation because food production at the subsistent levels had dried up.[19]

Davidson stated:

> By 2025, according to prudent conclusions, Southern Africa is projected to reach the level of urbanization that presently exists in the developed world and Latin America. About half of the population of eastern and western Africa will live in urban areas at that time. In absolute terms…this means that the urban populations of Africa will increase from four

to twelve times above their 1940 levels by 2025.

Worse: for if these huge urban populations cannot make food grow out of city streets, while rural producers do not improve on the statistically deplorable performance of the past decades, the necessary food will have to be imported: but there will be no money available to pay for such exports.[20]

Harewood argued that starvation is not only caused by adverse weather conditions but also by the abandonment of the land for the illusion of the better life in the cities. He felt that African leaders have ignored three crucial points in their economic planning: i) that an agricultural revolution should precede an industrial revolution, ii) that the city must not be developed at the expense or neglect of the countryside, and iii) food comes first.[21]

Leroy Harewood felt that golf tourism would compromise the food security of Barbados. He was not swayed by the argument that 'if this land is given over to foreigners for recreational purposes, we will get better foreign exchange returns than if we devote it to food crop or sugar production.' Harewood felt that 'taking arable land out of production is as pregnant with danger for the black man as the African slave trade.' He asked:

i) Who is going to own this foreign exchange, and how will it bring overall benefit to the country?

ii) How many golfers can we rely on permanently to use the facility, and how much will they contribute annually to the Government's coffers?

iii) How many persons will this golf course employ?

iv) Is it correct to assume that Barbados is such a great place that golfers from all over the world, their pockets crammed with Yankee dollars are falling over themselves to rush to these delightful shores to disgorge their money?

v) Who is to say that these golfers will not tire of Barbados, and on one dismal day take the next plane to Puerto Rico?[22]

Harewood was clear that what was needed in Barbados is an agricultural revolution not a proliferation of golf courses. Agriculture offers far more potential in helping the poor to rise above poverty and misery:

A poor farmer with a single cow and two acres of land is always going to be a man with more self-respect and dignity than a caddy on a golf course fetching and carrying the tourist bags. Moreover, 1200 acres of yams and potatoes are a far better insurance against starvation than 2000 acres of manicured grass.

In any case, we do not have the quantity of land in Barbados that would enable us to surrender vast portions of it to pleasure seeking individuals and the idle rich. Every year we import into this island 300 million dollars of food. A considerable portion of this food could be produced locally. But we need to exert ourselves, to upgrade and concentrate more efforts on the development of our agriculture. Most importantly we must retain our best land and manage our water resources intelligently if we have any intention of reducing the scandalous import of potentially dangerous food to feed an unwary people.[23]

According to Harewood, the attempt to 'discourage the development of agriculture in Barbados must not be seen as an isolated phenomenon, but it must be viewed as part of a wider problem rooted in the acquisition of quick money with little sweat. This mindset is rooted in the dependency syndrome.'

The need for a new political culture

Harewood was extremely unhappy with the existing Barbadian political culture. He believed that for too long Barbadian politics has been 'centered on bread and butter questions.' 'Our leaders have never exhorted us to become pioneers, creators and innovators.' The mendicant mentality of waiting for outside assistance and investments- part of the legacy of colonialism had become entrenched. This mendicancy has narrowly restricted our vision to a few consumer goods and we have largely ignored the wider issues of culture, education, the ownership and distribution of wealth in Barbados. In order to break out of this spiritual prison, according to Harewood, we must look beyond the basic questions of bread and butter, and seriously analyze our society with its class and racial divisions; its trade union leaders and politicians; its priest and teachers; its newspapers and radio; its banks and insurance companies; its merchants and planters, nothing must escape our study.[24] He raised a number of questions in the late 1960s that still have some currency today:

1) Why for instance in spite of all the talk about diversification of agriculture, we are still plagued with a one-crop economy?

2) Why is so much of our arable land still in the hands of white backward and ignorant planters?

3) Why do we continue to ape the Europeans in wigs and gowns in the running of our country?

4) What is the meaning of all these foreign banks in our country?

5) Why are so many of us constantly trying to escape from our color?

6) Why has the United States set up war machines on our soil?

7) Why do we allow Yankee racists like Ted Armstrong to poison the minds of our people with filth?

8) Why do we allow two essential public services like the Telephone and Electric companies to be controlled by foreign interests?[25]

Harewood felt that these questions have much to do with the 'respect and dignity of our people.' How they are answered will ultimately determine 'whether we advance or retrogress; whether we remain as pariahs of the human race or progressive people running successfully our own affairs' and getting the best out of the life of our people. That is why the concept of a 'New Politics' was sorely needed, not only in Barbados, but also throughout the West Indies, 'one that goes beyond bread and butter issues and personalities, but politics that is forcefully, ruthlessly progressive.' The kind of politics that will bring a new awareness in the mental outlook of the people, by releasing them from the 'dog eat dog' attitude of petty and selfish accumulation for immediate spending. 'The political authorities in Barbados and the Caribbean instead of answering these questions attack those who expose poverty, cultural decadence, ignorance and backwardness. He wondered how long a people can fool themselves.' 'How long can a people tolerate leaders whose vision does not extend beyond the corned beef tin and rum bottle?'[26]

Harewood argued that Grantley Adams was never a revolutionary and his party certainly does not believe in revolutionary struggle to seize power from the big land owning class and merchants and place it in the hands of the workers. He strengthens this point by stating that

Dr. Francis Mark said that Adams considered socialism a revolutionary and destructive philosophy. Certainly there is nothing that Adams has done to demonstrate that he has changed this political outlook. Therefore Harewood sought to shatter the myth that was being perpetrated by Harold Lidin and others, that the Barbados Labour Party (BLP) and the Democratic Labour Party (DLP) the two major political parties in Barbados, appear to share a similar attachment to a 'middle of the road' version of socialism and the only difference between the parties were personalities rather than platforms. According to Harewood 'there is no middle of the road socialism; a party is either socialist or it is not.' Therefore the BLP and the DLP are non-socialist parties prepared to follow the same paths that were inherited from British colonialism. 'Their idea seems to patch up and not to smash and build.' Like the majority of Pan-Africanists and socialists around this period he felt that the transformation of the people could only take place under a socialist system: the 'hopes and aspirations of our people' could only be met 'under a genuine socialist system, which would conquer the miserable legacy of poverty and backwardness.' It is only under a socialist system that the longing hopes of our people for a better life will be realized.[27]

Failure of the political leaders

Harewood mentioned that the time had come for the removal of Grantley Adams from the Barbadian political landscape (Grantley Adams was the first Premier of Barbados and the first and only Prime Minister of the ill fated West Indian Federation. He was also the leader of the Barbados Labour Party). He accused Grantley Adams of being a reactionary who sent an openly hostile cable to the British Government in 1953, against the progressive Cheddi Jagan's government in Guyana. One must remember that the Marxist Cheddi Jagan and his People's Progressive Movement were close allies of Harewood and the PPM. The cable read:

> Our experience of Jagan and his sympathizers leads us to feel certain that social and economic progress in the British West Indies is more likely to be harmed by that sort of person than by the most reactionary. However much we regret suspension of the constitution we should deplore far more the continuance of a government that put communist ideology before the good of the people.[28]

Moreover, what was more damning was when Adams gave a spirited defense of colonialism in Paris, in October, 1948 before a meeting of the United Nations General Assembly. According to George Padmore, Adams said:

> Colonial exploitation is a thing of the past... There may have been a time when "Colonialism"...was synonymous with exploitation. There was undoubtedly such a time. But today we are living in the twentieth century... Speaking therefore on the behalf of the peoples of the British Colonial Empire I reject categorically the notion that the out look for us is one of grim, relentless struggle for freedom against reactionary colonial oppressors.[29]

His actions forced the *West African Pilot* to write 'Mr. Adams by his irresponsible and uninspired utterances has dealt a wicked blow to all suffering peoples. We can ensure that neither history nor the African conscience will be kind to him when, at long last, the black men of the world come to their own.[30]

The *Observer* published by the progressive Wynter Crawford was also very severe on Adams:

> Mr. Adams ought to know that the overall policy of the Colonial Office stands condemned before all men of goodwill. Mr. Adams, by his irresponsible and inspired utterances put into his ignoble mouth by his British masters, has dealt a wicked blow at all suffering peoples...[31]

Like the *West African Pilot,* and the *Observer* Harewood felt that Barbadians could not be kind to Adams or any other group of discredited politicians. There is no time for sentimentality Adams and his friends had ample time to solve the problems of this country. Like Barrow and his friends Adams and his group must go and be replaced by real, solid revolutionary leadership and socialist leadership- a leadership that only the Peoples Progressive Movement can provide.[32]

Harewood did not confine his criticisms to Grantley Adams and the BLP alone but he also launched a broadside against Barrow and his administration- for not being faithful to its promise of building a 'Just Society.'(Errol Barrow was the third Premier of Barbados and the first Prime of Barbados. He was the leader of the Democratic Labour Party.) The 'Just Society' was interpreted by Harewood to mean just in equal opportunity, just in social relations, just in the sight of the law and just in freedom. However, he recognized that the Barrow government could not find any cure to the social and economic problems (rising prices, underemployment, unemployment, and poverty in the slums) facing the masses. Although the Barrow government was continuously 'sending begging missions to the U.S for aid,' the above conditions continued to exist. Therefore, Barrow began to widen the tax net and placed taxes on Caribbean immigrants, stoves, and type writers in order to raise additional revenue. Harewood opined that it is a cruel trick to pretend that the poor can be helped by taxing these items since there are not luxuries. He felt that every Barbadian should have a proper stove and poor girls learning to type needed additional typewriters.[33]

While the record of Barrow was a dismal failure on the domestic scene, its record on foreign affairs has been a little short of disastrous according to Harewood. Because it: i) continues to allow Yankee bases to remain on our soil, ii) refused to open diplomatic relations with socialist countries —including our neighbor Cuba (it should be noted however that Barrow started diplomatic relations with Cuba in 1972 and we will never know to what extent these charges led by Harewood and PPM influence this decision), iii) recognize the highly puppet regime in Taiwan instead of the People's Republic of China on the mainland, iv) has no real diplomatic and cultural relations with any African country, and v) refused to condemn the US bloody war against the Vietnamese people, or its racist policy against the Afro-Americans. Harewood concluded that never before has an independent nation looked so much like 'a colonial outpost of Yankee imperialism.' It seemed like the Barrow government was fearful of adopting an independent foreign policy. And many persons in Barbados and abroad were of the view that the island was a satellite of Western imperialism. For these 'misdemeanors' Barrow and his government must go! For they have forfeited the right to govern. The time has come to remove the old guard from their dominant position in West Indian politics. He believed that there is only one choice- we must accept a radical alternative to Barrow and Adams or we perish.[34]

Harewood blamed the leaders in Barbados for many of the shortcomings that affected the island. He stated that 'the bitter truth is that our failure of a people is rooted in the type and quality of what we have produced from the onset of colonialism to the present.' The 'Caribbean leaders of the 1930s had a most glorious opportunity to carry out a West Indian revolution,' but 'they failed and as a result many of the vexed economic and social problems that should have been settled then are still with us to this day.' He posited:

> While it would be entirely wrong to confine the achievements of the leaders of the 1930s to the dust-bins of history, yet these achievements were essentially peripheral and reformist. They did not reach down into the gut of society. Indeed, political leaders such as Grantley Adams and trade unionist Frank Walcott did not even hint about the economic enfranchisement of the dispossessed.
>
> What many called the assault on the oligarchy was little more than a tickle on its coattail. Black Barbadian leaders in the 1930s were essentially men without any serious working-class ideological commitment. They were good men in their way, but they had no sense of history, no sensitivity to the question of race and color. They wanted to seek peace with a ruthless and bigoted planter- merchant class rather than roll it in the dust...
>
> There were the occasional socialists like Charles Duncan O'Neal...yet all of those great names as they were individuals...working for the masses rather than for a complete reconstruction of Barbadian life.
>
> Thus, the social unrest of the 1930s was an abortive revolution. Very little has happened to restructure our economic and political system. The crying need for land reform was ignored. There was no basic change in the educational system, which was copied largely from England and was totally

unsuitable to the victims of colonialism. Even...
adult suffrage had to wait until 1951.

Grantley Adams and his friends, who assumed
office in 1946 under the banner of the Barbados Labour Party, were men still tied hand and foot to the
British Colonial Office. And it was doubtful if they
really wanted to break the chains that shackled them
to their white masters.

Lacking an essential political philosophy,
schooled in the idea that English traditions and English culture were the foundations of eternal excel-
lence, they have nothing to offer the people—nothing but a continuation of the old order. The idea, that
these black men in the House of Assembly had real
power was a delusion. True, they dressed and talked
and walked like their masters in the House of Commons in London. Like monkeys, they imitated every gesture, every insignificant detail of the British
Parliamentary System, but they still remained fakes
what one writer called mimic men.[35]

Harewood argued that the same questions that haunted
the people during the Adams era continued to haunt the
people under the Barrow administration.

• Scores of poor landless workers without any hope of
ever acquiring land.
• Rural decay and serious environmental problems.
• Vast Lazarus layers of permanent unemployed or
underemployed.
• Lack of a clear philosophy of education.
• No concerted effort to develop a viable agriculture
industry.
• No assistance to give quality assistance to potential
black businessmen.[36]

Harewood asserted that Barrow had no plan for refurbishing the dignity of Blacks and no plan to help blacks establish meaningful institutions and power bases for their development.

Leroy Harewood held the view that something was radically wrong with Barbados – 'our entire cultural, political and economic system is gangrene.' Ninety-five percent of the arable land is in the hands of a few people. All the banks with the exception of one are foreign owned. The insurance companies, the electric company, the telephone company and a considerable number of hotels are owned by foreigners and many of these foreign businesses are given over generous tax concessions and the benefit of docile cheap labour. From the days of slavery the black toiling masses have provided the wealth of this country without sharing in the fruits of their labour. 'While a few scraps have been thrown to the people to keep them quiet, the bulk of the wealth is created to enrich a handful of families.'[37] He made the firm assertion that this system must be changed because:

> We must know that this system was responsible for the slave trade-the selling of human flesh and blood. We must know that it is responsible for the one crop economy of all the West Indian islands, which in turn has enriched the white colonists and kept in indescribable poverty millions of black men.
>
> We must know that it has been responsible for the arrogance of the white man as has been the seed bed of racism; we must know that those who are trying to keep it intact are a handful of parasites who fatten on human degradation and misery.[38]

Harewood's position and the position of the radical left of the PPM closely mirror that of Fanon their ideological mentor:

Capitalist exploitation and cartels and monopolies are the enemies of the underdeveloped countries. On the other hand the choice of a socialist regime, a regime which is completely orientated towards the people as a whole and based on the principle that man is the most precious of all possessions will allow us to go forward more quickly and more harmoniously, and thus make impossible that caricature of society where all the economic and political power is held in the hands of a few who regard the nation as a whole with scorn and contempt.[39]

After cataloguing the ills of the economic and political system, Harewood concludes that Barbadians must find the ways and means of changing our society and releasing the talents and energies of our people to work for themselves and not for North American or British capitalists. He suggested that big business in Barbados must be taken over and run in the interest of the people. 'The plantations that have caused so much human suffering and misery should be liquidated and the land redistributed to the agricultural workers.' For Harewood the land question was fundamental, it was so during the 1876 Rebellion and it was critical in 1968. Indeed, he dismissed the popular interpretation of what occurred during the 1876 Confederation Disturbances, he felt that the political and constitutional issues were secondary; 'the disturbances were really about land for the landless agricultural workers, who were mercilessly robbed and oppressed by the planters.' To support this position he contended that some of the rebels openly stated: 'Well Kendal is a good estate and so is Colleton, but I think I'll take Pool.' The *Herald* newspaper of 1894 pointed out that the Confederation Disturbances was supposed to mean the portioning out of land - at least that was the general impression amongst the labourers. Harewood posited that the major 'problems facing the masses from 1876 to 1968 have not yet been resolved.' While the workers faced white terror in 1876, they now had the added component of 'white terror and black treachery in politics.' The 1876 uprising had an important lesson; that people will not tolerate oppression forever.[40]

Harewood was convinced that 'there is no justice in a society where some parents are forced to pay forty-five dollars per term for their children at bogus schools while others receive free education at better schools.' 'There is no justice in a society infested with unemployment, where women are driven to stealing or prostitution to get a meal for their hungry children while their so-called leaders argue about where to eat.' He pleaded with the leaders to listen to the voices of the people in the slums crying for work, food and shelter. Moreover, listen to cries of the agriculture worker as he 'struggles to make his pittance of $7 dollars and 84 cents to feed and clothe his ragged family.' Harewood strongly supported the sugar workers strike of 1968, and he advanced the case as to why all Barbadians should show solidarity with these workers. He wrote that:

> The sugar workers are among the most ruthlessly exploited people in Barbados. They worked pitiable long hours; their wages are low by any standards and they lived in wooden shacks cluttered in swamps all around the sugar plantations…
> No worker in Barbados should amble to work while the hand of the oppressor is at his brother's throat on sugar plantations.
> The clerk, the teacher, the water front worker must not delude themselves that they are apart, they are workers, and it is their duty to support other workers. Let them come out and support other workers. Let them come out and support their unfortunate

brothers on these slave plantations.
Workers of Barbados, Unite now in your interest, you
have nothing to lose but your poverty and fear![41]

Harewood was very disappointed with the outcome of
this labour dispute. He was of the view 'that never before
in the history of politics and trade unionism have so many
been deprived of so little in the interest of a small clique of
tight fisted money grabbers.' The workers did not receive
the $4.80 cents per day out of crop wages they were de-
manding, what they got was the legislation of $13.44 cents
for a 3 day week. What was perplexing to Harewood in this
matter was the fact that the trade union boss allowed a government that is the pliant tool of big business, to use this
legislational hoax on the workers. Why did the trade union
boss accept such a disgraceful compromise? Surely, the
Union boss must know that just as he cannot live on $13.44
cents per week (even if it is guaranteed by the Government)
the sugar workers cannot live on it either, unless of course
he wants them to continue to eke out a living far below the
poverty line.

Harewood argued that cane cutters could 'see through
the sham legislation and those who wanted to pose in their
interest.' The Barrow administration sought to convince
the sugar workers by a series of political meetings that the
Democratic Labour Party had broken the hands of the plantation owners by forcing them to pay the workers $ 4.48
cents a day for not less than a three day week. However,
many of the workers were not swayed by these meetings
and many of them were of the view that they were sold out
by the Democratic Labour Party. How can Barrow guarantee that they will really be employed for these numbers of
days when his government is powerless to stop the contin-
ual rise in prices? It is one thing to pass laws to implement
them is another. Harewood stated that the workers should

call on the Union boss to work for less than $13.44 per week or give up his position. They should also demand the same vigorous conditions for the Prime Minister and his toadies; for since they are servants of the people they should not receive higher salaries than the people.[42]

Harewood continued to repeat his call for the removal of the old guard from their dominant position in West Indian politics. He felt that the only choice left was a radical one to both Barrow (the DLP leader) and Adams (the BLP leader) or we will perish.[43] Harewood believed that for independence to be meaningful it should bring some transformation in the socio-economic conditions of the masses. Therefore on the eve of Barbados' second anniversary of independence he posed a number of questions to Mr. Errol Barrow the Barbadian Prime Minister.

1) Why have your government done so little to solve the economic and cultural problems facing our people?

2) Why have you stood idly by and allowed an organized band of robbers to fleece our people with high prices for our goods?

3) Why has your government refused to make a mark by tearing down the festering slums where thousands of people lived in appalling squalor?

4) Why under your administration as well as under the reactionary Grantley Adams before it, there has been no significant change in the massive number of unemployed now standing at over 20,000 persons?

5) Why do you continue to follow the old colonialist patterns of politics and economics?

6) Why do you allow the Yankee bases to remain on our territory occupying valuable land that could be used in the interest of our people?

7) Why does your government still persist in shipping so many of our women to be domestics in racist North America?

8) Is it Sir, that you and your bunch of men around you have no plan for advancing the people of this country?[44]

Harewood held the view that the Barrow government like the Adams government, its predecessor, was 'blind, weak and too timid,' to bring about any fundamental change within the country. According to him the flags, buntings, the colored lights, the extra dollar for pensions and the African dancers were all aimed at 'masking the discontent that was present.' Like Fanon, he felt that independence has brought fat salaries for a few lackeys and parasites; however it did not realize any tangible transformation in the lives of the largest segment of the population. Independence was therefore:

> only a fancy dress parade with the blare of trumpets? With a minimum re-adoption, a few reforms at the top and down there at the bottom an undivided mass, still living in the Middle Ages, endlessly marking time.[45]

Moreover:

> True liberation is not the pseudo-independence in which ministers having a limited responsibility hobnob with an economy dominated by the colonial pact.[46]

Harewood challenged Mr. Barrow to come and go with the PPM to see the wretched condition of the masses especially those persons living in Bridgetown.[47]

> See the hungry children scraping the garbage heaps among the flies and the rats for rotten bits of bread and fruit. See the rich waited on by hand and foot

by some badly paid houseboy or girl. See the smug
look on their faces of the fact that the merchants
who mercilessly plunder our country. See the white
plantation owners sitting under their umbrellas
watching black men and women toil in the fields for
a mere pittance. See the young girls drift towards
some sordid North American or British tourist. See
the plush banks hauling in our money to enrich
foreigners while our country remains in the grip of
stagnation.[48]

Smashing the colonial/neo-colonial state

Harewood continued to express the need for the restructuring of Barbadian society: politically, economically, socially,
educationally and even legally. While Barbadians may boast
about the institutions that we have inherited from our slave
masters, 'the bitter truth is that many of these institutions
cut at the pride and self respect of a people.' 'There is no
way a colonized people could accept wholesale the traditions and beliefs of their masters and hope to liberate themselves.' As Fanon succinctly stated:

> So comrades let us not pay tribute to Europe by cre-
> ating states institutions and societies, which draw
> their inspiration from her.
> Humanity is waiting for something other from us
> than such imitation, which would be almost an ob-
> scene caricature…
> For Europe, for ourselves and for humanity, com-
> rades, we must work out new concepts, and try to
> set afoot a new man.[49]

Moreover, Cabral said:

We don't accept any institution of the Portuguese colonialists. We are not interested in the preservation
of any structures of the colonial state. It is our opinion that it is necessary to totally destroy, to break,
and to reduce to ash all aspects of the colonial state
in our country in order to make everything possible
for the people.[50]

Harewood noted that the colonized people of North
America, who were of the same ethnic stock as the British,
sought to create new institutions and discarded the national
symbols and relics that would have reminded them of metropolitan Britain. Harewood reminds us:

Over in North America, after the American Revolution of 1776, when the thirteen colonies were set
free from British colonial rule, someone suggested
that the new flag of the independent states should
carry a cross similar to the British flag. This idea was
fiercely opposed, the new states wanted no symbol
or relic of their former masters to tarnish the new
nation.
Far from the retention of the British monarch as
Head of State, the American revolutionaries worked
out a brand new political system with an elected
president as their Head of State. The leaders of the
new American nation were proud, determined men,
prepared to develop a new nation free from the trap-
pings of a system that they found to be oppressive
and reactionary.[51]

What was paradoxical, shameful and hurtful was that
the descendants of slaves after independence could keep all
of the institutions that were responsible for their degrada-

tion. Harewood wondered 'how Barbadians could reconcile the acceptance of an imperial honor proclaiming the glories of the British Empire with the liberation of the African personality?' 'What kind of convoluted logic is this that would allow the representatives of an oppressed people to swear allegiance to a foreign monarch, her heirs and successors?' To Harewood this seemed like an act of lunacy, he cited the example of Tony Benn who refused the Queen's offer to change his name to Lord Stangate, although his father was a peer. In fact, he mentioned that Benn was engaged in a protracted fight to have the House of Lords dissolved. What was reprehensible according to Harewood, was not one single person in Barbados whose fore parents had been victims of slavery refused an imperial knighthood.[52]

Harewood was deeply concerned that with the dawn of the 21st century, black Barbadians most of them the offspring of African slaves, could be engaged in a debate as to whether or not the Queen should be retained as the Head of State. He mentions:

> How come since 1776, white men on that side of the Atlantic were so proud, so self confident, so resentful of British colonialism that they could develop a new political and legal system with only the faintest resemblance to the British, while black men are unable to show the mettle that would truly distinguish them as a people capable of developing systems relevant to their needs and dignity?
>
> People sometimes conveniently forget that we are the victims of British colonialism, and that the system of colonialism was based not only on the ruthless exploitation of human labour but also on the systematic degradation of its victims. To associate, therefore, with features of this system in a way that puts or maintains its chief representatives

as important national symbols is to undermine national respect and to weaken the psychic power of the people.

Barbadian political leadership… has never really understood the importance of the national psyche in nation building. These men have never grasped the crucial fact that in order to achieve real economic and cultural progress, in order to develop national consciousness and confidence, it is important to have a healthy psyche.

The acceptance and reverence of foreign symbols and institutions weakens and deforms the thinking of the people, thus they minimize their own achievements and importance or relegate them to the background of national or racial life.

It seems that many black Barbadians are suffering from a deep psychic sickness…In other words they still have serious problems accepting this blackness.

That is why the island's beauty contests tend to be won, not by the blackest girls but by those that are brown in complexion or nearer to the European standard of beauty…

The struggle to remove the British monarchy therefore, from the Head of State of Barbados must not be taken lightly. It goes to the very heart of our national life. It is about our pride and dignity as a people. It is about clearing our thinking and cleansing our social environment from the debris and dead weight of the past…

Firstly, any monarch assumes that there are vast differences in society based on wealth, blood and ancestry and that certain people have an ordained right to rule while others have a duty to follow like sheep.

...It has no place in a modern state aiming to create an egalitarian society based on merit rather than on ill-gotten fruits of hereditary.

Queen Elizabeth is the symbol of class and other social divisions in British society. It is not quite true that she unifies the nation. The very reverse is true. She is seen as a person who does not work and yet lives in opulence.

Barbados is still largely a plantation society; still a society fighting to keep itself, from falling apart in racial strife that has its genesis in the slave system and colonialism. The British Queen is therefore totally unsuitable as a person or symbol national unity; she can help to perpetuate the memory of a terrible ordeal of the past. Over two hundred years ago, the American revolutionaries realized that a monarchical system of government militated against national cohesion. Is there nothing we can learn from their experiment?[53]

Harewood remembered 'growing up stupid under the Union Jack,' when he sang with great gusto 'Rule Britannica for Britons never shall be slaves;' without knowing that he was not a British citizen and he had come out of the 'womb of slavery.' He blamed the school and the church for not telling him he was an African, and his fore parents came to the West Indies as slaves. These two pillars of socialization acted in cahoots with the colonial power to maintain a certain level of ignorance within society. He argued that institutions are created by individuals in a particular epoch to serve a particular class, or race in society, and those who slavishly copy them do so at their own peril. He opined 'our House of Assembly is a caricature of the British House of Commons.' They used that institution to help them maintain African slavery and to ensure European hegemony.

'The British Parliamentary system was also a class ridden system and never reached down to truly involve the masses in the decision making process of the nation.[54]

Harewood felt that the political system in the Caribbean was too remote and removed from the people. It is a system that purports to represent the people, while hiding from the people. He believed that the House of Assembly as it is presently constituted will have to be drastically reformed and the people will have to be organized at the community level. According to him 'the day of the big political party machinations and its army of opportunists and yard fowls must be rooted out.' The people must be educated. They must be able to think, to analyze and to solve the most pressing problems in their society. Harewood observed:

> Third World politicians coming into power in the wake of the decay of colonialism inherited a state apparatus from their colonial era. The third world politicians did not seek to restructure the state and to use its power to advance the cause of the people.
> Thus from Africa to Asia, from Latin America to the Caribbean, we find a criminal abuse of state power by a political class…
> This political class used the power of the state in the following ways. Firstly, they convert the state into a financial mulch cow, they legislate fat salaries for themselves. They also give themselves big allowances for cars, housing, travel and entertainment. So that at the end of the day their pay cheques are out of proportion to an average clerical worker in government. Yet many of these politicians have no skills or talents for anything.[55]

Weaknesses of the liberal democratic model

Harewood posited that 'parliamentary democracy must mean more than copying the British system, more than fat salaries, cruises on yachts, dainty meals and empty sounds about freedom and justice.' It should examine the growing poverty that was taking hold of the Caribbean and seek to create new paths in the face of difficulties. He was very critical of the system of Westminster Democracy as was practiced in Barbados. This was best manifested in the City by-election of 1969 when comrade Glenroy Straughn ran for the Peoples Progressive Movement (PPM). The PPM saw his election as a barometer to gauge the extent to which the masses had taken to their programme. The PPM platform was centered on bad housing, unemployment, land speculation and tourism. The PPM worked tirelessly in seeking to win this seat to give them a foothold in the politics of Barbados. However, the result left Leroy Harewood feeling very bitter and disappointed, since Glenroy Straughn only received a handful of votes, therefore he wrote:

> Should the political ignorant, the debauched and the corrupt who are prepared to sell their votes for a few cents be in the a position to determine the destiny of progressive people who honestly and sincerely believe in the economic, social and cultural advancement of their country?
>
> The recent by-election in Bridgetown is a clear and alarming example of how a backward populace for whom politics is a joke can be used to prop up and perpetuate a rotten system. Of how a people who are not prepared to analyze or question the faults in their society can and will always be used as a battering ram against the forces of enlightenment. All of course in the name of the shibboleth called democracy.

What democracy? Can we truthfully say that an ignoramus and mental cripple like poochum who worship at the shrine of Mottley and who waves a few dollars in the air given to her by her political bosses is a fit and proper person to cast a vote?

Why should some mindless drunkard who boasts about receiving gifts for his vote be allowed to go the polls and put an X against his name?

This is not democracy. It is madness. A people without political education not knowing their political behind from their head are a people who will continue to vote for the Mottleys, the Adams and the Barrows.[56]

Moreover, he stated:

The city by-election is now history. The people have cast their votes, the political hacks and termites are now at rest waiting in their holes and slime until they are called forth again by our noble rulers to perform yet another task of misinforming, corrupting and perverting the minds of the people.

The masses have made their decision ignoring the facts and figures and pour scorn on the progress of the city and sold themselves down the stench hole. They seemed to prefer misery and squalor, unemployment, starvation, homelessness and raggedness, ignorance and filth to enlightenment, cleanliness and economic and social advancement.

Who could imagine that in 1969 a mere 31 years away from the close of the century a people could be so politically backward that they could elect as their representative a man completely devoid of any zeal, courage or revolutionary ability to stand up and fight against the mountainous injustices that bedevil this country? Who could imagine that in 1969 a people could be so wicked as to inflict on themselves the son of a man who is a slum lord and shares the same golden conservative and anti-working class philosophy as his father.

The People's Progressive Movement presented a candidate that offered the city a unique chance to make a change from the sort of misrepresentation they had for over 23 years. Every social and economic question that affected them was answered by the PPM. In fact, never before in the history of this island had a political party done so much to open the eyes of the people to the harsh realities of life.

Yet they refused to awake and move forward. The Mottleys and the Adams and Barrows are good at giving them illusions.

What we of the PPM tried to do was to make the people understand the truth and stop the pretence and make-belief. We failed because of the deep inferiorisation of our people. And in this respect the people have also failed.

Maybe, says the optimist, the time is not ripe. Maybe, says the pessimist, the people are not ready to advance. But the question is when will they be and will it be too late?

For the vote given to Mottley is already a vote that pushes them nearer to the economic gallows.[57]

According to Glenroy Straughn, Harewood felt more disappointed than the candidate who lost the election, indeed he said 'this election left Leroy Harewood a broken man;' to the extent that he quietly retreated from the core of PPM activities and left the island to pursue academic studies in England.

Anti-imperialist

Harewood recognized that there was discourse in Barbados that stated if the U.S firms invested money in Barbados the socio-economic conditions of the unemployed and poverty stricken people would improve. Indeed, some narrow sighted persons were of the view that if Barbados was a colony of Uncle Sam, all our economic difficulties would disappear overnight. He warns that we must not allow ourselves to be deceived by thinking that U.S investments will usher in a season of plenty, and those languishing in poverty will suddenly awake to find their pockets crammed with Yankee dollars. He asserted that the reverse will take place since U.S investments: i) will exploit our cheap labor and turn our island into a more racist society; ii) will aggravate our economic position by making us more and more dependent on goods from the North American market which is one of the most expensive markets; and iii) that any progressive government that would attempt to make U.S business subservient to the interests of the people would be attacked by the U.S marines as was the case of the Dominican Republic in 1964, where under the pretext of protecting U.S business and citizens, Johnson rushed in his troops and brutally crushed a potentially progressive government that would have carried drastic economic policies in the interest of the people.[58]

Harewood unlike the political leaders in Barbados and the wider Caribbean did not see U.S interest bringing any humanitarian benefits to Barbados. He believed that U.S interest is political, economic and military. It is economic as far as the abundance of docile cheap labor is concerned. It is political to see that no government comes on to the scene that will be hostile to capitalism and imperialism; and military in using the territory as a base to help defend her Atlantic seaboard or to launch aggression against socialist countries or any country that seeks to overthrow puppet governments that are not working in the interest of the people. Harewood argued that any one who has studied the history of Cuba would have seen that although there were massive investments in that country poverty levels were extremely high and the infrastructure was underdeveloped. Attendant features of U. S investments are the surrendering of our country's sovereignty and the prostituting of the rights of the people. This is a price that none but the corrupt, the servile or the ignorant would be willing to pay.

Leroy Harewood as a rabid anti-imperialist argued that Barbados must stridently adhere to the doctrine of 'friends of all and satellites of none', the statement that Prime Minister Barrow made when Barbados was admitted as a member of the United Nations. Therefore Harewood and the PPM strongly opposed Barbados becoming a member of the Organization of American States. The OAS was viewed as a tool of neo-colonialism. Harewood advanced the argument that the OAS countries were some of the most heavily exploited countries in the world, with millions being ravaged by Yankee imperialism. Moreover, Cuba was kicked out of the OAS because its revolutionary government sought to break the stranglehold of U.S. big business in Cuba. According to him 'the people of Barbados were not interested in stopping Castro but they were interested in stopping Yankee imperialism.' Harewood felt that no tangible benefits would accrue to Barbados because it was a member of the OAS, since Barrow 'only joined the OAS to get protection from his U.S. boss if and when the people of this sad island rise up against his rule, like the other corrupt regimes that are murdering the people of Latin America with Yankee bayonets and protection.'[59]

Harewood was highly critical of British imperialism, and was extremely happy that the British Empire had started to collapse and Britain was in a state of decline. The

British economy was under severe stress, 'her armed forces known for slaughtering people worldwide was run down and her industrial structure built by child labor and the African slave trade was now archaic.' This former superpower sacked and pillaged other nations in her bloody wake of empire building was now reduced to a beggar. Britain was forced to seek a loan from international bankers to prop up the pound sterling. However, many Englishmen believed that Britain was still a major power and could continue to play the role that it played before. Harewood avers that even Harold Macmillan the former British Prime Minister must admit that the British lion is becoming far too weak to devour the unwary in Africa, Asia and the Caribbean. However, he cautioned 'that it would be wrong to dismiss British imperialism completely for although U.S. imperialism is rapidly replacing the British in areas like Africa and the Caribbean; the grip of the British lion still possess a great threat to the advancement of the people.'[60]

Clement Payne/NDP alliance

Harewood as a member of the Clement Payne Movement and the National Democratic Party (NDP) alliance (1993) continued to agitate for a new political culture that differed from the old political culture of the established political parties. Like many Barbadians he was quite optimistic that the NDP would bring a breath of fresh air to the Barbadian political landscape. However, to Harewood's dismay the NDP seemed to be heading down the road of the established political parties? Therefore Harewood challenged Dr. Richie Haynes for the Presidency of the NDP in order to reverse this development if he was successful. He stated:

The leadership of the NDP is defective... because the leader is trying to make the Party another DLP. He doesn't want any, real fundamental changes- he wants to model himself as a Barrow and this is his fundamental mistake. So he's trying to go along the same elitist road, hostile to people who dare challenge his leadership...A leadership that went down in humiliating defeat in the last election- an elitist group that has not learned one iota from that defeat. And my challenge therefore for the leadership of the party is because if you build a new party, and you are sincere, you have got to chart a new course. You cannot follow blindly the Barbados Labour Party or the Democratic Labour Party.

I am not concerned about what people called the expansion of education; I'm concerned with the quality of education. You certainly have secondary schools, you have a lot of primary schools but what are they teaching? How do black people see themselves in relation to other people? What programmes are in place to ensure that black people can hold their heads high and go places? That Blacks can control the commanding heights of their economy?...And you will notice that no politician in Barbados, and certainly (not) in the Black Diaspora, have addressed this problem. But nobody has ever addressed this mental sickness of Black people.

A good example is what is happening at Thickets, Three Houses, Montcrieffe, in St. Phillip and Guinea Plantation in St. John. Recently we were told that these plantations have decided to go out of production because they don't have enough money to pay the people, well the workers would have seized those plantations as simple as that...The land belongs to the people... They are workers; they have always been the workers. These are the people who worked the plantation for years...and you can start by controlling a political party...as the cutting edge for genuine advancement of people. And it is against this type of background, therefore, that I see myself as becoming a leader of a political party, to use it as a cutting edge to bring about the deep seated transformation that is necessary in Barbadian society.[61]

Leroy Harewood was unsuccessful in his quest for the Presidency of the NDP and he left the party shortly thereafter because he could not be part of the old political order.

Pan-African solidarity

Harewood like Nkrumah believed that the greatest danger facing Africa is neo-colonialism, and its major instrument balkanization. According to Nkrumah:

Neo-colonialism is based on the principle of breaking up former large united colonial territories into a number of smaller non-viable states, which are incapable of independent development and must rely upon the former imperial power for defense and even internal security. Their economic and financial systems are linked, as in the colonial days, with those of the former colonial ruler.[62]

Harewood felt that the Nigerian civil war was a painful reminder to African leaders who had not yet grasped the significance of Kwame Nkrumah's words. There can be no victory for the General Gowon camp or the Colonel Ojukwu in a weak and divided Africa. The British and the French imperialists were supporting different sides in the conflict out of their own self-interest. Nigeria is extremely rich in mineral resources including oil, manganese ore, silver, and monazite and tin, the imperialists are after these minerals. He blamed the African leaders not only in Nigeria, but also across the continent for not uniting to stem the white tide of imperialism and racism.[63] The civil wars in Sudan, Zaire and Ethiopia, like the Nigerian one, were all aimed at further balkanization of the continent.

Like all Pan-Africanists, Harewood was very concerned with the ongoing developments in Southern Africa; he felt that when Britain, the United States and other so-called Western democratic countries talk about freedom and the free world they do not include the non-white peoples. He felt that the brutal killings in Rhodesia must be seen in the same light, as the mass killings of the Vietnamese peoples by United States, both Lynden Johnson and Ian Smith are guilty of crimes against humanity. However, the white men believed they are engaged in a 'so-called holy war against communism, therefore their crimes are covered over with meaningless platitudes.' He felt that non-white people especially the Africans have got to learn that the time for platitudes was over. 'If we are not to go the same route as the American Indian, we have got to put into practice the adage of an eye for an eye and a life for a life.' Because for too long white fascist/racist regimes in Southern Africa and the United States have gotten away with murdering black people for very trivial offences, therefore he felt that it was high time for these hangmen to get a dose of their own medicine.[64]

Harewood recognized that the Western powers were very hypocritical on the question of Rhodesia. While they speak about the use of force and sanctions in the United Nations against Rhodesia, 'behind their backs they pass a slimy hand to Ian Smith for filthy lucre.' In the words of Alex Douglas Hume the former British Prime Minister 'it was simply a matter of white kith and kin versus blacks.' He argued that the British Government was too morally decrepit to apply force so they have stressed economic sanctions, Britain, France, Germany, Belgium, Switzerland were still trading with Rhodesia. Harewood felt that the Africans are reading the signs of the times because small guerrilla forces are beginning to penetrate into Rhodesia. The sooner a total show down come the better, because nothing but violence can tear the leeches of Europe from the arteries of Africa and dash them to the ground. He stated:

> By now all Africa should have been a vast Vietnam making it far too hot for the racists to continue their bloody rule.
>
> The one and only sensible course of action left to the Africans is all out war or freedom. As long as Africans ignore or allow them to be diverted from the path, Ian Smith and his type shall continue to rule the roost in Africa.[65]

Harewoood in paying tribute to Malcolm X posited the view that 'Malcolm X's name is synonymous with the black liberation not only in the United States where millions are crushed under the boots of the racist terror, but, also in Africa and the Caribbean where a vast majority are forced into subjection by the forces of white oppression and tyranny.' He remarked that Malcolm X was determined to tear up the United States society in a bid for total liberation. Malcolm X had the courage, the ability and tenacity for this task and the racist whites were cognizant of this development and feared him. Therefore they set out to destroy him. Although he is dead, 'Malcolm's spirit lives on in black freedom fighters everywhere who are determined to march to victory whatever the price.'[66]

Harewood linked the struggle of the Caribbean students in Canada, at Sir George Washington University, against the racist professor, to the universal struggles of black oppressed peoples everywhere for freedom. He felt that the Caribbean students on trial in Montreal must make efforts to preserve the essential unity of their just cause, both among themselves and with the other brothers, sisters and comrades who are on the spot. And to guard against the spurious nationalism that would logically emerge during the conduct of the defense, he feared that this nationalism would cause balkanization and division. The idea of a Grenadian national, St Lucian national, Guyana national or any such national is hardly more than a spurious claim and is inimical to the genuine attainment and preservation of their basic human rights.[67]

Caribbean unification

The question of West Indian unification is a subject that is very close to the heart of all progressive West Indians, Leroy Harewood a committed Pan-Caribbeanist was very critical of the Caribbean Free Trade Area (CARIFTA), which he described as a 'large capitalist plan hatched to integrate the Caribbean market in the interest of the capitalists.' He argued that the merchant class in the Caribbean 'fought tooth and nail against the West Indian federation, because they thought that any strong unity coming from the people would damage their interest.' They were assisted in this fight by the 'ignorance, petty jealousies, bigotry and rivalries of the politicians.' These insular reactionary forces won the battle and smashed the hopes of millions of West Indian people who looked forward to a creation of a West Indian nation. However, these forces of reaction became cognizant of the 'difficulties of producing for small, inward looking, isolated markets and they have hatched out a rotten plan for economic integration.' To bring about the realization of their plan they have engaged the services of politicians 'whose vision stretched no further than the pork barrel and the rum bottle, politicians who have learned nothing and have forgotten everything.'[68]

The Caribbean people definitely need unification, but this form of capitalist integration (Carifta) is not what we want. Any integration must be worked out on lines that would bring maximum benefits to the masses and not to a handful of rich financiers. Carifta in the words of Harewood was 'no more than a vicious ganging up of the rich against the poor workers of this area.' Harewood asserted that Carifta would have to go and be replaced by genuine economic and political integration of the Caribbean along socialist lines. Like Arthur Lewis, he felt this development could only come to fruition when the present leaders of the West Indies were dead.[69]

John Connell, a member of Harewood's PPM, bluntly stated:

> The latest attempt to make the system work even more profitable for big business is the Caribbean Free Trade Area. The idea behind Carifta is simple, selfish and ruthless. The wealthy few big business-men in Guyana, Jamaica, Trinidad and Barbados, are eager to increase their wealth. To do this they must sell their over-produced, over-priced goods outside their shores to other territories.
>
> To get these into the victims' territories they must pull down certain trade barriers. To do this the wealthy merchants and industrialists must en-list the aid of the national leaders whom the people elected.
>
> In political terms what Carifta means is this: our rulers, that is to say the Big Six in each of our territo-ries are coming closer together aided by Britain and America. Our ruling class has never been interested

in Caribbean Political Union. At times in the past
they have fought openly and fiercely. Neither they
nor their foreign allies welcome a coming together
of the masses.[70]

Critique of the *Time for Action Report*

Harewood was highly critical of the *Time for Action Report*,
the latest study on Caribbean integration; he described the
document as 'dull, stale and boring.' The *Time For Action
Report* was put together by a group of eminent Caribbean
integrationists who traveled around the Caribbean and
the Caribbean Diaspora in North America and Europe, to
solicit the ideas of individuals and groups as to what was
needed to fast track the regional integration project; and to
insure that the Caribbean was not marginalized in the un-
folding world order characterized by mega blocs and free
trade. The report was called *Time for Action* to dramatize the
need to quicken the regional integration process. According
to Harewood if we are to believe that the main purpose of
this document is to help West Indians to meet the challenges
of the 21st Century, then it is a bitter disappointment. The
commissioners have almost taken us for a ride. Harewood
wanted to know how useful is this jumble of words to the
poor man in the streets of Kingston or Castries, who yearns
for a profound and qualitative change in his life? What help
is this report to the millions of misinformed and uniformed
people in the entire Caribbean, who have never been educated about the benefits of Caribbean unification?[71]

Harewood took the position that 'West Indian Unity
remains a chimera,' because West Indian societies are essentially intellectual and cultural waste lands. The people don't
know who they are, or where they want to go. On some
occasions they are more American than the Americans and
on other occasions they are more British than the British.

He recognized that 'political and economic unity can not be achieved in a waste land where every man is rootless and ethnically castrated.' Political unity demanded a single-mindedness of purpose and an ideology hammered out on the anvil of common struggle, common purpose and trust. He felt that the Caribbean people must be forced march into the 21st century. A thousand Commissions can never hope to achieve this. West Indian societies, present a painful patch-work of people constantly struggling for narrow individual ends. Therefore, the specter of 'individualism will militate against national or even racial unity, especially among the African sector of the population.' Moreover, if racial solidarity is so hard to achieve within a single territory, it will be definitely harder to accomplish across the wider West Indies.

Harewood described West Indian societies as fishnet societies. They let in people from outside the region - tourist or third rate investors. But those in the net- the natives, are trapped, unable to move very far, not only because of limited space but because they have come to feel and think that the net is still part of the ocean. They have not learned to swim around in their little nets, waiting to be thrown scraps by the big fishermen. He reminds us that 'historically West Indian societies have always been atomized.' The planters were never united on anything except chattel slavery, whilst the slaves found it extremely difficult to unite among them to fight the common enemy the slave masters. He argued that both the slave and ex-slave master came out of a tradition where there was a lack of self confidence and self-esteem. This lack of self-confidence and self esteem plays havoc with the psyche of West Indian people. West Indian societies are rotten to the core. And they have never been fully emancipated. However sophisticated those societies may appear with their modern school buildings; their university and university graduates; their ultra modern supermarkets and thousands of Japanese built cars, the majority of the people have not been able to free themselves from thinking like European; since there has been no profound West Indian thinking on anything.[72]

According to Harewood, the Report of the West Indian Commission failed to provide the type of sociological analysis that would tackle the deep-seated problems that affected the Caricom. He mentioned that Time for Action was just a cliché and the West Indies has no need for more commissions. What the people need is quality education to free their minds from centuries of backwardness and genocidal ignorance. Unite or Perish! Is far more meaningful than Time for Action.

Black middle class

It is generally accepted that rein of Barrow from 1961-1976, witnessed the emergence and the rapid expansion of the black middle class, living in the heights, terraces and parks, shopping in New York and Miami. While many commentators viewed this era as one of 'opulence,' Harewood emphatically stated, 'it was an era of greed and foolishness.' Because, the 'black middle class sold its soul for a mortgage and a car and lost its social consciousness in an ocean of pretence.' The Black middle class believed that it owned something, however it owned nothing. This point was strengthened by Hilbourne Watson who stated: that 'the fact that they do not normally own or control any significant quantities of capital stamps it with a mark of profound insecurity and uncertainty about its objective location in society and its future.'[73]

Harewood makes the point that the black middle class believes it was educated while it was mis-educated. It believed it had power, yet it remained pitifully powerless.

Indeed, this class even sought to deny its own history, its race, and despised the very class from which it had emerged. The perceptive Clennel Wickham in the middle 1930s wrote off the middle class as a broken reel and argued that the democratization of society would come only as a result of the organization of the working class people committed to their own self-emancipation.[74]   While Hilbourne Watson stated:

> In other words, the generally conservative outlook that permeates the existential consciousness of the black middle class is, I submit, a function of historical factor and ideological conditioning. Its defensiveness is a function of its insecurity; its almost pathological indifference to, and cynicism about, racism is a function of the implosion of its aspirations and the self-contempt expressed in the prevalent (myth) view that blacks cannot manage business; and the distance from the control of capital. All of these characteristics are reinforced by a profound absence of the critical appreciation of the history of Barbados, the history of the Caribbean and Africa's historical role in the world.[75]

Watson continues:

The black middle class clearly senses that it is different from the working class. In many ways, most in the middle class continue to have one foot in chattel housing. They are not comfortable with social analysis that incorporates or employs a methodology derived from or informed by social class analysis. The middle class tends to eschew race concepts and embraces social cohesion and values of universal national identity. This is the ideology of populism. The outlook is buttressed by pragmatism, cynicism and anti-communism. Progressive persons are labeled as radicals and forthwith ostracized. Bourgeois forms of mass consciousness are commonplace and a strong sense of national purpose is lacking.[76]

Revolutionary prospects of Barbadians

The period of the nineteen sixties was one of revolutionary fervor throughout the countries of the South, the ideas of the revolutionary theorists like Fanon, Guevara, Debray, Cabral and others were heavily debated in many intellectual and popular circles. It was the norm for revolutionaries to carry out various analyses to determine which section of the society had the most revolutionary potential (whether the peasants, working classes, lumpen-proletariat etc) therefore it was not unusual that Leroy Harewood one of the leading Barbadian revolutionaries of the period would put the microscope on Barbados and seek to answer this question for *Manjak* newspaper. Harewood felt that the progressives in Barbados must understand: i) the type and quality of change that we want, and ii) the tools we have or intend to use to bring about the restructuring of our societies. He took issue with some of the progressives in Barbados, including those in *Manjak*, for seeming to project the idea that the masses are sacrosanct. While he agreed that the black Barbadian masses have met with political betrayal from the planter merchant class and from the rising black bourgeoisie. He opined that it is extremely difficult to accept the view 'that the arrogance of the Bajan man in the street is proverbial, and this acts as a mental fetter preventing him from understanding the social and political realities of his environment.' His recent experiences with the PPM and *Black Star* had prevented him from seeing the 'god like blacks in Nelson Street, New

Orleans, College Bottom or Messiah Street as totally inno-
cent of helping to rivet the chains of their own ankles.' He
felt the fundamental question 'was how to get a people who
have been brutalized and humiliated by centuries of slavery
and colonialism to reject the vicious and reactionary forces
that have spawned in the last quarter century of the twentieth century?' According to him unless we understand that
at every level of our societies, political and cultural backwardness has enveloped both the working class and the (so-
called) middle class. The working class and the middle class
throughout the Caribbean are in need of strong political education. These classes must be taught the ABC of politics, of
history, and even the elementary principles of self-respect,
and human dignity, before they begin to even glimpse what
the radicals are getting at.[77]

Harewood noted that one of the most daunting challenges confronting the Left was how to educate or re-edu-
cate the people. He warned, 'don't fall into the trap of be-
lieving that naked oppression and poverty are sufficient to
awaken a people to a sense of struggle.' Moreover, don't believe that 'every member of the middle class is a traitor hell
bent on selling out the poverty ridden.' Harewood was very
pessimistic about the revolutionary potential of Barbadians;
this was borne out by his own political experiences and the
historiography of Barbados. 'Any schoolboy knows that
riots and big demonstrations are not the stuff from which
revolutions are made.' Like many Marxist-Leninists, he asserted that the masses do not make revolutions. Revolutions
throughout history have been made by groups of disgrun-
tled, determined, dedicated individuals who were prepared
to make enormous and unstinting sacrifices. They did not
depend on slogans and appeals to the mass mind alone but
set about to build a revolutionary party. It is nonsensical 'to
talk about a revolution, or to believe that a set of people are
revolutionary, because of a set of historical circumstances.'

What determines whether or not we are revolutionary can 'never be measured in terms of poverty, or of our ability to storm a law court against high telephone charges.' All of this is common, simple, pressure group politics—the flesh and bones of all liberal democratic capitalist states.[78]

Harewood noted that Calvin Alleyne and himself sought to demonstrate that the legacy of slavery and colonialism might have severely affected the psyche of the Barbadian people. Since colonialism deforms and warps the minds of victims, sometimes rendering them unfit to look beyond the narrow confines, of 'a nasty, hand to mouth existence.' Barbadian society has not undergone any fundamental change to escape Fanon's definition of a classic colonial society. The challenge in Harewood's view is 'for revolutionaries to search for solutions, not piece-meal social engineering; but rather using the scalpel on those gangrenous portions of the fabric of national life.' It was obvious that for too long the Caribbean Left allowed itself to be swamped with emotion instead of building effective organizations. Many of the so-called socialists and revolutionary Black Nationalists seem to imagine that by shouting revolution or giving some strange hand-shake or clenched fist salute that they are helping to make the revolution. Harewood posited that revolutionaries must learn to subject themselves to rigorous self-analysis. 'Nothing and Nobody must be spared.[79]

The essential difference between the optimist (optimistic about a revolution) and the realist (pessimistic about a revolution) is this: the optimist sees revolution in every demonstration, in every attack upon the establishment however insignificant, or from which section of the population it emanates from; the realist knows that revolutions are 'not brams' and are not made by that amorphous mass sitting night after night in the broken down rum shops of Nelson Street or Baxters Roads. These are potential rioters not revolutionaries. He asserted that revolutions are made in spite of these people and seldom with them. 'These are the people who are considered by objective social commentators as English rustics living in blissful ignorance living blissfully in festering squalor.'[80] He was adamant that:

> We cannot and will not shake off our past by ac-claiming it has no value. Nor can we build a new so-ciety, a new people on rotten foundations left behind by colonialists.
>
> If we are to move forward we must discover if we are in a state to undertake our journey. If this is not the case we must solve the problem and equip ourselves for the task. This is surely a more logical view than the other one, which would have us be-lieve that we can run when in fact we may neither, have the strength nor the will to crawl.[81]

It is instructive that while Harewood was influenced by Fanon, his position differed sharply from Fanon's on the role of lumpen-proletariat; he did not have a lot of faith in the lumpen-proletariat as a revolutionary force.

Recolonization

As a fervent anti-imperialist Leroy Harewood was dismayed when Barbados entered a Structural Adjustment Programme (SAPs) with the International Monetary Fund. Harewood knew that countries that have entered these programmes faced tremendous hardships and their sovereignty is lost as they operate under the dictates of these institutions. SAPs generally require the devaluation of currency, deregulation of prices and wages, reduction of public spending on social programs and state bureaucracies, removal of subsidies on food and basic necessities, liberalization of trade regimes, privatization of trade regimes, and the expansion of the export sector. Harewood described the IMF as an 'economic ninja' that is controlled by the United States Government, and is connected to 'bullying Third World countries' into adopting policies that make these countries sources of cheap labor and large profits for American businessmen.

Harewood fervently argued that it was incorrect to blame all sections of the Barbadian economy for the foreign exchange shortage confronting the Barbadian economy. He was adamant that the high consumption oriented lifestyles were not enjoyed by the working class, but had been wasted by the business elite, the wealthy members of the middle class and the government. Therefore it was quite immoral for any one to suggest that the burden of adjustment package should be borne by the masses. Harewood was of the view that the 'working class in Barbados should recognize that the government they had elected are now playing the role the local business establishment have been advocating for many years.' Therefore, what should be 'uppermost in the minds of the workers, is how they can organize to defend their rights and interest, which their forebears have struggled for?' What was obvious was the fact that the workers could not depend on the established political parties or the trade union leadership to fight this battle for them. Therefore the workers must devise their own restructuring program and they should not be railroaded into a program that will destroy all they strive for.[82]

Harewood was philosophically opposed to the privatization ideology- the attendant to the neo-liberalist philosophy. Indeed, he was disturbed by the discourse of the free market salesmen/women who preached that privatization was the panacea to all the economic ills confronting Barbados. He cynically stated:

> Ever since the brutal days of the Margaret Thatcher regime in Britain privatization has become an economic cliché.

The economic and financial wizards in our midst have taken to it like the populace have taken to Christianity.

Completely incapable of working out any formula to rescue the island from economic disaster, intellectually bankrupt and dependent on the throw offs from their masters in the great metropolitan centers; they now serve up privatization as the panacea to all of our woes.

They cry: Privatize the cement factory! Privatize CBC! Privatize the Transport Board! Privatize Heywoods and the Hilton! Privatize the Insurance Corporation of Barbados and the Pine Hill Dairy!

But why stop there? Go the whole hog. Privatize all government schools including the Polytechnic and Community College; Privatize the University; Privatize the Hospitals and Polyclinics and the Sanitation Services.

Privatize the Public Library, the Museum and Archives. Better still sell off all Parks, Beaches and Places of recreation. Privatize the roads.

And then cry, Hocus–Pocus! Like magic, all our problems will disappear in thin air, you see the smoke.[83]

Harewood was mindful that:

An examination of the historical record would show conclusively that extensive state intervention in industry, trade, finance and agriculture has been an almost universal feature of successful industrialization, both in the mature industrial countries and in those in the Eastern NICs that have real wage economies through industrialization.

Although such evidence cannot prove that intervention is necessary for successful industrialization, it does dramatically weaken the plausibility of the claim that such intervention is always an unwelcome source of distortion and inefficiency.[84]

In light of the collapse of the existing socialism in Eastern Europe and elsewhere and the triumphalism of capitalism; many supporters of capitalism were excited that this development had come to pass. Many felt that the world would now be a better place. However, Harewood the visionary being mindful of European history of the recent past reminded his readers that the destruction of semi-left wing governments has led to the development of extremely right wing and fascist's dictatorships. This was evident in Nazi Germany, Franco's Spain and Mussolini's Italy. He wondered, what would be the outcome of the present political disruption of Eastern Europe? Will Western and Eastern Europe eventually unite their economic systems for world dominance? Will the United States unite with them to build a world empire, the likes of which had never been seen before? Harewood opines:

> Non-European people living in small economically impoverished backwaters of the world must view a combined capitalized Europe and North America as a dreadful prospect. Millions of Europeans living on either side of the Atlantic have never felt particularly concerned about asserting their racial superiority over other ethnic groups. Indeed, much of the economic and political philosophy of Europe seems to be interwoven with racialism.[85]

He felt that the social Darwinist philosophy of Albert Beveridge and the neo-conservatives was very much alive. The resurgence of the neo-conservatives in the United States and Europe was very worrying to Harewood. In 1900,

Senator Albert Beveridge declared:

> God has not been preparing the English speaking
> and Teutonic peoples for a thousand years for noth-
> ing but vain and idle self-contemplation and self-ad-
> miration, No! He has made us the master organiz-
> ers of the world to establish systems where chaos
> reigns... He has made us adept in government where
> chaos reigns... He has made us adept in government
> among savage and senile peoples... He has marked
> the American people as His chosen nation to finally
> lead in the regeneration of the world...[86]

Harewood observed that since the collapse of socialism
the Euro-centric worldview had become more aggressive.
He recognized that the liquidation of the socialist states had
not ushered in the saner and safer world; on the contrary,
what he saw was a world where race, power politics, and
naked aggression against those who are considered to be
inferior will become the hallmark of the Bush New World
Order. Moreover, countries refusing to conform to U.S. dictates, run the risk of becoming economic and political pariahs, or worse, being wiped out by massive military action.
The political independence of small, weak states or even big
non-military states will be little more than a sham and not
even the resources of those countries are likely to remain
under their exclusive control. Harewood ominously warns:

> For us inferior races in the Third World, our eco-
> nomic and political position might deteriorate to
> the extent that we no longer have the right to de-
> cide anything. Economically and militarily weak,
> we could become little more than serfs feeding the
> maws of world capitalism with our blood, our sweat
> and our raw materials.[87]

Conclusion

Leroy Harewood was an uncompromising fighter on behalf of the oppressed in Barbados, the Caribbean and worldwide. Harewood fought valiantly for the political, economic, psychological, cultural and social liberation of all peoples of African descent, and all oppressed Third World Peoples. Beyond any shadow of doubt, he has made an invaluable contribution to Pan-Africanism and socialist thought in Barbados, as a journalist, teacher and an activist with the PPM, the Clement Payne Movement and the Pan-African Movement of Barbados. Therefore, it is imperative that we seek to canonize him and spread the word about this organic intellectual of Pan-Africanism.

Long Live Comrade Harewood, Long live!

Notes

[1] See Leroy Harewood, "Who are we?" *Black Star* (April 6, 1968).

[2] *ibid.*

[3] *ibid.*

[4] Leroy Harewood, "Who are we (2)?" *Black Star* (April 27, 1968).

[5] John Henrik Clarke, *Who Betrayed the African World Revolution* (Chicago: Third World Press, 1995) 86.

[6] Cheik Anta Diop, *The African Origin of civilization*, Trans. By Mercer Cook (New York: Lawrence Hill, 1974)231.

[7] Leroy Harewood, "Who are we (2)?" *Black Star* (April 27, 1968).

[8] *ibid.*

[9] *ibid.*

[10] *ibid.*

[11] Leroy Harewood, "Who are we? (5) *Black Star* (June 8, 1968).

[12] Leroy Harewood, "Hunger: Why is there Underdevelopment?" *Black Star* (February 8, 1969).

[13] *ibid.*

[14] Walter Rodney, *How Europe Underdeveloped Africa.* (Washington: Howard University Press, 1982)10.

[15] *ibid.,* 20-21.

[16] Leroy Harewood, "Hunger: Why is there Underdevelopment?"

[17] *ibid.*

[18] Leroy Harewood, "Africa: The Starving Giant." *Pulse.* (September 11-17, 1992).

[19] *ibid.*

[20] Basil Davidson, "African the politics of Failure," *Socialist Register* (1992) 214.

[21] Leroy Harewood, "Africa: the starving Giant."

[22] Leroy Harewood, "Golf Tourism or Agriculture," *Pulse* (July 10-16, 1992)

[23] *ibid.*

[24] Leroy Harewood, "Beyond Bread and Butter," *Black Star* (*September* 11-17, 1992).

[25] *ibid.*

[26] *ibid.*

[27]Leroy Harewood, "Adams and Co Must Go," *Black Star* (August 3, 1968).

[28] Leroy Harewood, 'This man must go,' *Black Star* (July 20, 1968).

[29] George Padmore, *Africa: Britain's Third Empire* (Negro University Press, 1966) 181.

[30] Leroy Harewood, 'This man must go,' *Black Star*, (July 20, 1968).

[31] Woodville Marshall, *The Memoirs of Wynter Crawford: I Speak For the People* (Kingston: Ian Randle Publishers, 2003) IX.

[32] Leroy Harewood, 'This man must go,' *Black Star*, (July 20, 1968).

[33] *ibid.*

[34] *ibid.*

[35] Leroy Harewood, "A bunch of pure jokers," *Pulse* (May 15, 1992).

[36] Leroy Harewood, This Man must go.

[37] Leroy Harewood, "What must be done," *Black Star* (December 30, 1967).

[38] *ibid.*

[39] Frantz Fanon, *The Wretched of the Earth.* Trans. By Constance Farrington (Harmondsworth: Penguin, 1984) 74.

[40] Leroy Harewood, "Lessons of 1876," *Black Star* (February 10, 1968).

[41] Editorial, *Black Star*, (February 24, 1968).

[42] Leroy Harewood, 'Sugar Workers no Victory,' *Black Star* (March 9, 1968).

[43] *ibid.*

[44] Leroy Harewood, "Shame!" *Black Star* (November 30, 1968).

[45] Fanon, 118.

[46] Frantz Fanon, *Toward the African Revolution.* Trans. Haakon Chevalier. (Harmondsworth: Penguin Books, 1970).

[47] Leroy Harewood, "Shame."

[48] *ibid.*

[49] Fanon, *The Wretched of the Earth*, 254-255.

[50] Africa Information Service, *Return to the Source: Selected Speeches of Amilcar Cabral* (New York: Monthly Review Press, 1973) 83.

[51] Leroy Harewood, "Fear of Change," *Pulse* (October 9-15, 1992).

[52] *ibid.*

[53] Pulse (July 3-9, 1992).

[54] Leroy Harewood, "The Future of Barbados," *Pulse* 3-9, 1992).

[55] *ibid.*

[56] Editorial, "Democracy," *Black Star* (June 7, 1969).

[57] Leroy Harewood, "A Vote to Break their Own Necks," *Black Star* (June 7, 1969).

[58] Leroy Harewood, "When will we ever learn?" *Black Star* (October 19, 1968).

[59] Leroy Harewood, "When will they ever learn?" *Black Star* (October 25, 1968).

[60] Leroy Harewood, "The End of an Empire," *Black Star* (January 27, 1968).

[61] Julius Gittens, "Democracy Myth blown Up!" *Sunday Sun* (May 20, 1993).

[62] Kwame Nkrumah, *Neo-colonialism: The Last Stage of Imperialism* (London: Nelson, 1965).

[63] Editorial, "Civil War in Nigeria: The Greatest Danger," *Black Star* (August 17, 1968).

Pan-African Humanist 145

[64] Editorial, "Murder and Platitudes," *Black Star*, March 1968 and the Editorial, "Rhodesia," *Black Star* (October 1968).

[65] Editorial, "Rhodesia," *Black Star* (October 19, 1968).

[66] Leroy Harewood, "Malcolm X in Retrospect", *Black Star (February* 24, 1968).

[67] Editorial, "Unity," *Black Star* (February 27, 1969).

[68] Leroy Harewood, "Will Carifta Cause unemployment," *Black Star* (June 22, 1968).

[69] *ibid.*

[70] John Connell, "Carifta for Big Business," *Black Star* (June 22, 1968).

[71] Leroy Harewood, "West Indian Unity Chasing a Chimera," *Pulse* (November 6-19, 1992).

[72] *ibid.*

[73] Leroy Harewood, "The Future of Barbados," *Pulse* (July 3-9, 1992).

[74] Leroy Harewood, "Why was Sandi Chosen?" *Pulse* (May 22, 1992).

[75] Hilbourne Watson, "Beyond Ideology: The Question of the Black Middle Class in Barbados," *Bulletin of Eastern Caribbean Affairs*, 16 No 6 (January/February, 1990).

[76] *ibid.*

[77] Leroy Harewood, "Are Barbadian Revolutionary People?" *Manjak* (April, 1974).

[78] *ibid.*

[79] *ibid.*

[80] *ibid.*

[81] *ibid.*

[82] Leroy Harewood, "New Vision, We're here to chart a new path," *New Vision* Vol.1 No.1 (July 1991).

[83] Leroy Harewood, "Straight Talk," *New Vision* Vol.1 No.2 (September, 1991).

[84] Manfred Bienfeld, "The New World Order: Echoes of a New Imperialism," *Third World Quarterly*, Vol. 15, No. 1. (March 1994) 42.

[85] Leroy Harewood, "The New World Order," *Pulse* (November 26-December 5, 1992).

[86] *ibid.*

[87] *ibid.*

An Appreciation

By Horace Campbell and Rodney Worrell

> Naturally if you ask me between brothers and comrades what I prefer- if we are brothers it is not our fault or our responsibility. But if we are comrades, it is a political engagement. Naturally we like our brothers but in our conception it is better to be a brother than a comrade. We like our brothers very much, but we think that if we are brothers we have to realize our responsibility of this fact and take clear positions about our problems in order to see if beyond this condition of brothers, we are also comrades. This is very important for us.
>
> -Amilcar Cabral, *Return to the Source*

The Caribbean and the global Pan-African world have lost a quiet and determined leader who had dedicated his life to the emancipation of all human beings. Comrade Ricky Parris was a Marxist, a revolutionary Pan-Africanist, a rhythm poet and a trade unionist. He had an undying love for the masses of black people and working people in Barbados and throughout the African world. This undying love for the masses was developed as a teenager when Ricky started to examine the existing unequal social order. Ricky dreamt of a world constructed on the principles of egalitarianism and he decided that he would do everything in his power to bring this society into being.

Ricky joined a number of progressive organizations both formal and informal in order to realize the society he envisioned. He became a member of Youth for Revolutionary Change, Movement for National Liberation and the Workers Party of Barbados (WPB). In addition, he also ran as a candidate on the WPB ticket in the 1986 General Elections. Ricky became a founding member of the Southern African Liberation Committee (SALC) one of the most progressive organizations to appear on the Barbadian landscape. This group was in the vanguard of raising Barbadian consciousness about the evils of the apartheid system in South Africa. His involvement with the SALC sharpened his political activism and sharpened his Pan-Africanism. He was also a founding member of the Pan-African Movement of Barbados; where he served with distinction as Chairman, Secretary and Treasurer.

The passing of Ricky Parris is a sad day not just for his family, the Barbadian working peoples, Caribbean peoples, but also for all of those who wanted decency and another form of human organization. Ricky Parris was an organizer and educator of the working peoples. After five decades of trade unionists who used the working class for personal political advancement, Ricky wanted the Barbados Workers Union to be an organization with integrity, fighting for the health, well being and security of all peoples of Barbados, those formally employed and those whose lives are distorted by the nature of neo-colonial capitalism.

Ricky Parris was one of the most sincere, passionate and decent political activists we have ever met. In the past, those who considered themselves to be part of the radical tradition did not live lives that could be examples of decency and honesty. More importantly, while Ricky had been exposed to the varying left political tendencies of the region his goal was to find a path that could end the history of enslavement and low regard for African lives.

Ricky always sought to raise the level of Pan-African discussions in Barbados; he organized a number of seminars so that PAMOB could engage the wider Barbadian public on Pan-Africanism. He also sought to promote public education through organizing the 'Black Night' sessions at various community centers. Ricky organized a meeting with Pan-Africanists at the Commission for Pan-African Affairs office because he wanted a full discussion among Pan-Africanists about the conditions of farm workers in Zimbabwe. For him the land question was of utmost importance since there were many poor Barbadians who were losing their land. He wanted to learn both the positive and negative lessons from the Zimbabwean experience. For him, while land reform was important, what was more important was the attempt to manipulate the working peoples.

Ricky Parris was a revolutionary Pan-African thinker who constantly grappled with the usefulness of Pan-Africanism in this conjuncture of rabid capitalism. He 'felt that many Pan-Africanists were trapped in traditionalism and have not recognized the powerful pull of globalization and the tactics needed for the battle in the twenty-first century.' According to him not all the fighters know how to go forward. He recognized that Pan-Africanism was a dynamic concept which was continually transforming itself, gaining new ideological perspectives in light of the challenges of the new global conjuncture. Ricky like Walter Rodney felt 'that Pan-Africanism should never become a sterile formulation in the hands of African petty bourgeoisie but must be used as an instrument to bring about the transformation of the masses.' Ricky in the mould of Frantz Fanon felt that Africans in the Diaspora should not be blinded by the inevitable pitfalls of romantic visions about the African continent and allow illusions to take the place of serious analysis. Critical to Ricky analysis was the question of the social forces represented in government and the level of social, economic and political transformations that had taken place in society.

Ricky took pride in the fact that the Barbadian peoples maintained the openness of the prime beach-front. He was against speculators. When we walked along the beach he pointed to a beachfront property that was being held by a prominent Caribbean entrepreneur. This entrepreneur had refused to develop the beachfront property because he could not violate Barbadian law by making this beach private. Ricky was well loved by all, we passed on our morning walks along the beach before we took a dip in the water. He would stop in at the fishing villages along the way and speak to the brothers and sisters who were either seafarers or those who were fishmongers. They all knew Ricky; he inquired about their health and their children.

Ricky had an undying love for working people. This was manifested when he took up the mission to organize a group of farmers into a cooperative project. This venture was proving to be a real challenge in getting the support and cooperation of the farmers, some members of PAMOB felt that Ricky should give up and be contented with his efforts but Ricky persisted and displayed a revolutionary patience very similar to the biblical Job. He felt that he should never give up on the farmers and that one day they would see the wisdom of forming the cooperative. Moreover, Ricky brought an agricultural specialist to the island to address many of the problems confronting the farmers and to show them why a cooperative was an imperative for their survival. Ricky also held discussions with the vendors association as to how best PAMOB could assist them in their protracted struggle against harassment by the government authorities.

Ricky wanted to reflect on the traditions of struggles in Africa and the Caribbean that could break the present forms of Babylonian oppression. He was against war. He was against drug dealers and he was a cultural worker who had the pulse of the people. His rhythm poetry ensured that his voice and message reached a wider constituency beyond the traditional employed workers and beyond the meetings of the PAMOB. Where ever he performed persons requested that he did his two monster hits "Shipwrecked" and "They can never stuff it out." These pieces captured the essence of Ricky's Pan-Africanist philosophy. Ricky organized the first ever Folk Fest for the PAMOB where he sought to use another medium of reaching the Barbadian public. Ricky also led the Barbadian delegation to PAN-AFEST in Ghana 2003; where he thrilled many with his dynamic performances. He was particularly happy about going to Africa especially Ghana as this was the first time he was visiting the mother land.

Ricky was a Pan-Africanist in words and deeds. He was at the center of all the activities of the PAMOB, since the mid-nineties as Chairman, Secretary and Treasurer. Indeed he was seen as the organizer within the ranks of PAMOB, he always played a leading role in the yearly trek to Farley Hill National Park to proclaim/re-proclaim it as the Mandela Freedom Park. In the mid-nineties a group of Pan-Africanists calling themselves the Free South Africa Committee made a call to the Barbadian Government to have Farley Hill National Park rename the Mandela Freedom Park, in recognition of Mandela's commitment to the liberation of his people. Every year PAMOB reminded the Barbadian public about this call and the need to bring about its realization. This event was also important as the members of PAMOB would start to plan the program of activities for the year. Ricky also played an integral role in organizing the yearly program at Bayley's to commemorate the 1816 Bussa Rebellion; the Black Nights' sessions of poetry and conscious raising discussions; the educational programs within PAMOB on many topical issues. Ricky was beyond a shadow of a doubt the leading ideologue within PAMOB between 1998 and 2005. One of the last things we discussed was mobilizing for the Walter Rodney Commemoration groundings in Guyana (13-15 June 2005). It was his dream to have another Pan-African Conference of Caribbean Pan-Africanists and he felt that the Rodney Conference could be the launching pad of such an initiative.

His love for Africans did not include hostility to other peoples. He opposed all forms of chauvinism. He could not understand politicians who spoke of Caribbean unity, supported the freedom of Caribbean entrepreneurs, but opposed the freedom of movement of Caribbean workers. He wanted all races in the Caribbean to live in peace.

His opposition to capitalism meant that he was not opposed to Europeans as human beings, but opposed to those who refused to accept the crimes committed in the name of spreading civilization.

Ricky has left an important legacy for all of those who want peace and justice. Long live my Brother! Long live my Comrade! Long live my mentor! Long live my friend!

Select Bibliography

Abdul Raheem Tajudeen, *Pan Africanism: Politics, Economy and Social Change in the Twenty-first Century*. New York: New York University, 1996

Africa Information Service, *Return to the Source: Selected Speeches of Amilcar Cabral*. New York: Monthly Review Press, 1973

Amadiume Ifi, *Daughters of the Goddess: Daughters of Imperialism*. London: Zed Books, 2000

Amin Samir, *Eurocentrism*. New York: Monthly Review Press, 1989

Bernard Magubane, *The Ties That Bind: African American Consciousness of Africa*. Trenton: Africa World Press, 1978

Campbell Horace, (ed), *Pan-Africanism :The struggle against imperialism and neo-colonialism: Documents of the Sixth Pan African Congress*. Toronto: Afro-Carib Publications, 1975

Campbell Horace, *Militarism, Warfare and the Search For Peace in Angola*. Pretoria: Africa Institute, 2001

Campbell Horace, *Reclaiming Zimbabwe: The Exhaustion of the Patriarchal Model of Liberation*. Trenton: Africa World Press, 2003

Capra Fritjof, *The Turning Point: Science, Society and the Rising Culture*. New York: Simon and Schuster, 1982

Chossudovsky Michel, *The Globalization of Poverty: Impacts of IMF and World Bank reforms*. London: Zed books, 1997

Clarke Henrik John, *Who Betrayed the African World Revolution*. Chicago:Third World Press, 1995

Cohen Cathy, *Boundaries of Blackness: AIDS and the Breakdown of Black Politics*. Chicago: University of Chicago Press, 1999

Diop Anta Cheik, *The African Origin of civilization*, Trans. By

Mercer Cook. New York: Lawrence Hill, 1974

Eglash Ron, *African Fractals: Modern Computing and Indigenous Design*. New Brunswick :Rutgers University Press, 1999

Esedebe P.O., *Pan Africanism: The Idea and the Movement*. Cambridge: Harvard University Press, 1982

Fanon Frantz, *Black Skin, White Masks*. New York: Grove Press, 1967

Fanon Frantz, *Toward the African Revolution*. Trans. Haakon Chevalier. Harmondsworth: Penguin Books, 1970

Fanon Frantz, *The Wretched of the Earth*. Trans. By Constance Farrington Harmondsworth: Penguin, 1984

Geiss Immanuel, *The Pan-African movement: A history of Pan-Africanism in America, Europe, and Africa*. New York: Africana Publishing House, 1974

Goonatilake Susantha, *Toward a global science : Mining Civilizational Knowledge*. Bloomington: Indiana University Press, 1998

Gourevitch Philip, *We Wish to Inform You that Tomorrow We will be killed along with our families: Stories from Rwanda*. New York: Farrar, Straus and Giraux, 1998

Harding Sandra G, *The 'Racial' Economy of Science: Towards a Democratic Future*. Bloomington: Indiana University Press, 1998

Hochschild Adam, *King Leopold's Ghost: a story of greed, terror, and heroism in colonial Africa*. Boston: Houghton Miflin, 1998

James C.L.R, *A History of Pan African Revolts*. Chicago: Charles H Kerr, 1995

Jinadu Adele (ed) *The Political Economy of Peace in Africa*. Harare: AAPS, 2000.

Lemelle Sidney J and Ifi Ni Owoo, *Pan Africanism for Beginners*. New York : Writers and Readers Publishing, 1992

Lubiano Wahneema, *The House That Race Built: Black Americans, U. S. Terrain*. New York: Pantheon Books, 1997

MacLean Barbara Hutmacher, *Strike a woman, Strike a rock: Fighting for Freedom in South Africa*. Trenton: Africa World Press, 2004

Mamdani Mahmood, *When Victims Become Killers*.Trenton: Princeton University Press, 2001

Mandaza Ibbo and Dan Nabudere (ed) *Pan Africanism and Integration in Africa*. Harare: Sapes Books, 2002.

Marable Manning and Leith Mullings (ed) *Let Nobody Turn Us*

Around: Voices of Resistance, Reform and Renewal, New York: Rowman and Littlefield Publishers, 2000

Maren Michael, *The Road to Hell*. New York: The Free Press, 1998

Marshall Woodville, *The Memoirs of Wynter Crawford: I Speak For the People*. Kingston: Ian Randle Publishers, 2003

Mkandawire Thandika, *Our Continent, Our Future: African Perspectives on Structural Adjustment*. Trenton: Africa World Press, 2000

Nkrumah Kwame, *Neo-colonialism: The Last Stage of Imperialism*. London: Nelson, 1965

Nkrumah Kwame, *Africa Must Unite*. New York: International Publishers, 1972

' Nyong'o, P. **Anyang** (ed.), *Popular Struggles for Democracy in Africa*. London: Zed Books, 1988

Ousmane Sembene, *Gods Bits of Wood*. Portsmouth: Heinemann, 1978

Rifkin Jeremy, *The Biotech Century: Harnessing the Gene and Remaking the World*. New York: Putman Books, 1999

Roberts Dorothy, *Killing the Black Body: Race, Reproduction and the Meaning of Liberty*. New York: Vintage Books, 1999

Rodney Walter, *How Europe Underdeveloped Africa*. Dar Es Salaam: Tanzania Publishing House, 1972

Shiva Vandana, *Biopiracy: The Plunder of Nature and Knowledge*. Boston: South End Press, 1997

Sparks Allister H, *Tomorrow is Another Country: The Inside Story of South Africa's Road to Change*, New York: Hill and Wang, 1995

Thompson Vincent B, *Africa and Unity: The Evolution of Pan Africanism*. London: Longmans, 1969

Thiongo Ngugi Wa, *Decolonizing the Mind*.Portsmouth: Heinemann, 1986

Vandervort Bruce, *Wars of Imperial Conquest in Africa, 1830-1914*. Bloomington: Indiana University Press, 1998

Veal Michael E., *Fela: The Life and Times of an African Musical Icon*. Philadelphia :Temple University Press, 2000

Wamba Phillipe, *Kinship: a family's journey in Africa and America*. New York: Dutton, 1999

Walter Rodney Speaks:The making of an African Intellectual. Trenton: Africa World Press, 1990

Watkins William H, *Imaging Home: Class, Culture and Nationalism in the African Diaspora.* London: Verso Books, 1994

Witte De Ludo, *The Assassination of Patrice Lumumba.* New York: Verso Books, 2001

Woodson Carter G, *The MisEducation of the Negro.* Trenton: Africa World Press, 1990

Worrell Rodney, *Pan-Africanism in the New Global Conjuncture: Has the Internationalization of Capital Rendered this Concept Irrelevant?* Miami: Universal Publishers, 2003

Worrell Rodney, *Pan-Africanism in Barbados.* Washington: New Academia Publishing, 2005

Webliography

http://academic.udayton.edu/race/02rights/reparaOo.htm
http://africanaction.org
http://afrikan.net
http://www.africanhistory.net
http://www.allafricanpeoplesrevolutionaryparty
http://www.assatashakur.org/forum
http://www.arm.arc.uk
http://members.aol.com/aaprop
http://www.inpdum.com
http://thetalkingdrum.com
http://.transafricaforum.org
http://www.theblacklist.net
http://www.thedrum.org
http://www.panafrican.info
http://blackculturalstudies.org/m_diawora/panafr.html
http://igcs.binghamton.edu/igcs_site/dirton6.html
http://info-ghana.com/Pan-africanismhtm
http://diaspora.northwestern.edu
http:www.extent.org/Politics/Mim/countries/Pan-African/index.htm
http://www.millionsforreparations.com
http:www.national.org/reparationshtm
http: www.ncobra.com
http://theblackcommentator.com
http://www.afger.com/nationalism
http:emancipationtt.org
http:www.blackradicalcongress.org/education.html
http://www.thetalkingdrum.com

http://reparationscenter.hotmail.com
http://www.reparationsthecure.org
http://directblackaction.com
http: www.swagga.com/reparation.htm
http:www.nbufront.org
http://marcusgarvey.com
http://blackquest.com/link.htm
http://eblackstudies.org/intro/chapter15.htm
http://www.unia-acl.org
http://pambazuka.org
http://www-sul.stanford.edu/depts/ssrg/africa/history/
hispanafrica/html
http://www.brothermalcolm.net/index.html
http://www.cwo.com/zlucumi/runoke.html
http://raceandhistory.com/historicaliews/2002/22022.htm

Index

160   Index

www.ingramcontent.com/pod-product-compliance
Lightning Source LLC
Chambersburg PA
CBHW031202270326
41931CB00006B/378